Caribbean Connections

Puerto Rico

EDITED BY
DEBORAH MENKART AND
CATHERINE A. SUNSHINE

LESSON PLANS BY
CATHERINE A. SUNSHINE AND
ERLAND ZYGMUNTOWICZ

Ecumenical Program on Central America and the Caribbean (EPICA)
1470 Irving Street, NW
Washington, DC 20010
(202) 332-0292

Network of Educators on the Americas (NECA)
1118 22nd Street, NW
Washington, DC 20037
(202) 429-0137

Introductions and lesson plans © 1990 by the Ecumenical Program on Central America and the Caribbean (EPICA) and the Network of Educators on the Americas (NECA) (formerly the Network of Educators' Committees on Central America, NECCA.)

Book design by The Center for Educational Design and Communication, Washington, DC

Readings separately copyrighted (see acknowledgements).

Library of Congress Catalog Number: 90-062779
ISBN 1-878554-04-2

Printed in the United States of America

Second Printing, 1992.

Contents

Introduction

A RETIRED COUPLE FROM Ohio taps their meager savings for a three-day cruise to the Bahamas. Shirts sold in a Dallas department store carry labels saying "Made in the Dominican Republic." Grocery stores a mile from the White House stock hard-dough bread, coconut tarts and ginger beer for a clientele of 30,000 Jamaicans living in and around Washington, DC.

The Caribbean, along with Mexico, is the Third World region closest to the United States. Its history is intertwined with ours in a multitude of ways. Thousands of Americans visit the islands each year as tourists. Persons of Caribbean origin make up one of the largest immigrant groups in the United States and Canada, and their number is growing. Extensive aid, trade and investment link the U.S. to the Caribbean economically. And the United States has intervened repeatedly in the region to influence political change.

Despite these close links, most Americans know little about Caribbean societies. The region is often depicted as a vacation playground—a paradise of "sun, sea and sand" for the enjoyment of tourists, but not a place where real people live and work. Political and cultural developments in the region often go unreported in the U.S. media. When the Caribbean is discussed, racist and anti-communist stereotypes often blur the images.

As a result, many Americans have missed the opportunity to know the proud history and rich cultural traditions of this neighboring region. Caribbean people have overcome many obstacles and realized outstanding achievements in political, economic and cultural life. The mingling of diverse peoples has produced cultures which are vibrant and creative, and which have enriched U.S. and Canadian societies through the migration of Caribbean people north.

Until recently, most school curricula in the United States included little information on the Caribbean. Textbooks often mention the region in passing during discussion of Latin America. There are few secondary-level resources widely available in the U.S. wl ch are up-to-date, historically and culturally accurate, and which view Caribbean realities through Caribbean eyes.

These packets were prepared to enable schools to begin incorporating material on the Caribbean into existing curricula. They are not a substitute for developing curriculum units on the Caribbean, a project which

remains to be done. It is hoped that they will help spark interest in teaching and learning about the Caribbean, which will lead to the development of more comprehensive teaching resources.

▼ Objectives and Methods

Four aims guided the editors in their selection and presentation of materials:

• To show Caribbean history and contemporary realities through the eyes of ordinary people, both real and fictional. Oral histories, interviews and other forms of first-person testimony provide a people-centered view of Caribbean life. An example is the autobiographical essay by Minerva Torres Ríos (Unit 2), in which the author recalls her personal experiences of growing up in Puerto Rico and migrating to New York.

• To promote critical thinking rather than simply the memorization of information. All writing contains a point of view, which may be stated or implied. If students examine values and unstated assumptions in whatever they read, they become active participants in their own learning. Where a topic is controversial, we have attempted to include several viewpoints, as in the discussion of Puerto Rico's political status (Unit 9). The student is asked to weigh the evidence, and perhaps to do further research, before drawing his or her own conclusions.

• To stimulate students' interest by creatively combining different types of materials, such as short stories, novel excerpts, nonfiction essays, interviews, newspaper clippings, song lyrics, poetry and drama. Unit 3 on the *bomba* and the *plena*, for instance, includes essays by scholars on the origins of the music, song lyrics in Spanish and English, and reflections by musicians on what the music means to them.

• To ensure the authenticity and relevance of the material. We sought suggestions from Caribbean people and organizations in the Caribbean, the U.S. and Canada, and relied on an advisory council of Caribbean scholars for ongoing review. There are hundreds of Caribbean civic organizations, and many academics and teachers of Caribbean origin, in North America; they can serve as a primary resource for developing a program of study on the region.

▼ How to Use These Materials

This packet is one of six in the Caribbean Connections series. It is aimed principally at grades nine through twelve, but may be adapted for use at higher and lower levels. The readings, discussion questions and

suggested activities are intentionally varied in their level of difficulty. The instructor is encouraged to select those parts for which the content and level are compatible with curricula in use.

The packet begins with a brief history of Puerto Rico, which provides a framework for the nine units which follow. Each unit includes a lesson plan, an introduction, and one or more readings. The lesson plans are for the instructor's use; they include objectives, discussion questions and suggested activities. The introduction sets the context for the readings; it may be handed out to students, or the instructor may present the information orally. The readings are intended as student handouts.

Each unit also suggests resources for further study. Although varied in difficulty, these tend to be at a higher reading level than the readings included in the packet. They will be particularly appropriate for assigning special research projects to individual students or small groups. Addresses for publishers and other sources of materials are included in an appendix.

It is important to note that these packets are not a curriculum, that is, a self-contained program of study. They do not attempt to provide a complete introduction to the Caribbean or to individual Caribbean countries. They present, instead, materials which can be used to supplement curricula in areas

such as Social Studies, English or Third World literature, African-American or Latin American history, Spanish, Multicultural Studies or Global Education. If an instructor wants to devote a full unit of study to the Caribbean or to a certain country, we recommend that s/he use the packets in conjunction with other materials.

The secondary social studies curriculum of most school districts does not devote a significant time directly to the Caribbean. However, this should not discourage teachers from using these materials. There are many opportunities to address the region within the scope and sequence of traditional social studies and language arts curricula.

The major ways of integrating the Caribbean are through the study of (a) United States history, (b) social studies themes, (c) current events, and (d) language arts (especially Spanish and English). Many of the lessons could be introduced as students are studying the history of the United States or the Western Hemisphere. For example, Unit 1, A *Lead Box Which Couldn't Be Opened*, might be incorporated into a course on 20th century United States history during discussion of the Korean War. Units 4 and 6 provide a colorful description of the daily life of many working women and men in the 19th and early 20th century. Unit 5, on Arturo Alfonso Schomburg, can be used in studies of important people in our nation's history.

The Caribbean can illustrate many required social studies themes and issues. For example, Unit 2, *Memories of Puerto Rico and New York*, can provide the basis for a discussion on the causes and impact of immigration. Unit 1 touches on the draft, colonialism and cross-cultural conflicts. Unit 3, on traditional Puerto Rican music, shows how diverse influences form a country's culture. Unit 7, on Operation Bootstrap, can be used in studies of development and the environment.

The world affairs section of the newspaper is often discarded in favor of sports or comics because current events seem "so confusing." The confusion arises because the media often reports on events in isolation, apart from their historical context. By learning about the roots of conflicts or issues, students develop the ability to interpret and analyze news reports. All of the lessons in this packet provide background to understanding the debate presented in Unit 9 on Puerto Rico's political status. The personal testimonies allow students to imagine what position they might take if they were Doña Licha or Minerva Ríos. Students will begin to see that opinions on political issues are not reached abstractly, but depend on an individual's or community's historical and current experiences. Students using this packet may develop their own opinions about Puerto Rico's political status. But it is equally or more important, in terms of developing global

respect and cooperation, that students come to understand the diverse positions taken by Puerto Ricans.

Some of the units provide opportunities for students to develop and express their own opinions. As part of Unit 7, students can write letters of opinion or request additional information from the Du Pont Company. While studying Unit 9, students may wish to contact their Congressperson to inquire about his or her position on Puerto Rico's political status. If the school is in a community with Puerto Rican organizations, various classes could be combined and a panel convened to present different viewpoints on the issue.

This packet also lends itself to cross-disciplinary studies. Many of the readings can be used more than one course, such as social studies and music, or English and Spanish.

The present series of packets is a first edition and will be revised based on feedback received. The editors would be pleased to hear from instructors and students who have used the materials. We want to know how the materials are being used, which parts have proved most effective in the classroom and which need improvement. Contact: Caribbean Connections, P.O. Box 43509, Washington, DC 20010. (202) 429-0137.

Acknowledgements

DEVELOPING THIS PACKET involved many people, and was largely a labor of love. We are grateful to Rina Benmayor of the Centro de Estudios Puertorriqueños (Center for Puerto Rican Studies) at Hunter College, City University of New York, for her valuable advice at every stage. Oral history materials developed by the Centro form the backbone of several units. Néstor Otero, an artist working with the Centro, and Nélida Pérez and Amílcar Tirado of the Centro's library staff assisted with graphics research.

Filmmaker Susan Zeig kindly provided English and Spanish dialogue from the film *Plena Is Work, Plena Is Song.* The National Ecumenical Movement of Puerto Rico (PRISA) supplied materials from interviews done by their staff in Puerto Rico. Virginia Wilkinson's 12th grade class at Abington Friends School in Jenkintown, Pennsylvania carried out a thorough review of the draft from a student perspective.

We wish to thank the Center for Educational Design and Communication, a project of the Religious of the Sacred Heart, for their excellent work on production. Melanie Guste, RSCJ, created the design which brought the materials alive. Kathy Davin, a teacher at the District of Columbia's Oyster Bilingual School, provided critical assistance with research, editing and proofreading. Laura Margosian and Kimella Ledbetter typed much of the original manuscript. We thank Sally Harriston, a teacher at Wilson High School in Washington, DC, for her help in administering the project.

The D.C. Community Humanities Council provided the initial grant for the Caribbean Connections series. Other support came from the CarEth Foundation and the Anita L. Mishler Education Fund.

THE PUBLISHERS would like to thank the following for their permission to use copyrighted material:

José Luis González for "A Lead Box That Couldn't Be Opened/ *Una caja de plomo que no se podía abrir,*" translated by permission of the author; the Centro de Estudios Puertorriqueños and Minerva Ríos for "Memories/ *Remembranzas,*" from *Nuestras Vidas: Recordando, Luchando y Transformando;* the Centro de Estudios Puertorriqueños and Carmen Clemente for "The Traditions of My People/*La persona humilde de Puerto Rico,*" from *Nuestras Vidas: Recordando, Luchando y Transformando;* Jorge Arce and Kris Eppler for the interview with Jorge Arce; Juan Flores and the Centro de Estudios Puertorriqueños for "Bumbún and the Beginnings of La Plena," adapted from an article in *Centro,* Vol. II, No.3; Susan Zeig and Pedro Rivera for "Plena Is Work, Plena Is Song/ *Plena, Canto Y Trabajo,*" from the film by the same name; Monthly Review Press for "The Customs and Traditions of the Tabaqueros ..." from *Memoirs of Bernardo Vega* edited by César Andreu Iglesias, New York, 1984; Valerie Sandoval Mwalilino and Epifanio Castillo Jr. for "Arturo Alfonso Schomburg: Our Forgotten Scholar," from *Nuestro,* May 1978; the Schomburg Center for Research in Black Culture, The New York Public Library/Astor, Lenox and Tilden Foundations for "Schomburg and the Harlem Renaissance," by Victoria Ortiz; the Centro de Estudios Puertorriqueños for "Our Mothers' Struggle Has Shown Us the Way," from the audio program "*Nosotras Trabajamos en la Costura/* Puerto Rican Women in the Garment Industry"; South End Press for "Doña Licha's Island," from *Doña Licha's Island: Modern Colonialism in Puerto Rico* by Alfredo López, Boston, 1987; the National Ecumenical Movement of Puerto Rico (PRISA) for the interview with Purita Gil Pérez, from *De Prisa,* August 1986; the National Ecumenical Movement of Puerto Rico

(PRISA) for the interviews with Severino Rivera Morales and Angel Ventura Cintrón, from *Vieques and Christians*, Bayamón, Puerto Rico, 1981; *Latinamerica Press* for "Vieques Island Dwellers Take Over Navy Land" by William Steif; TransAfrica for the interviews with Baltasar Corrada del Río and Wilma Reverón-Tío, from *TransAfrica Forum*, November 1982; the office of Jaime B. Fuster for the interview with Jaime B. Fuster.

Every effort has been made to locate copyright holders for the granting of permission. The editors would be glad to hear from anyone who has been inadvertently overlooked in order to make the necessary changes at the first opportunity.

▼ GRAPHICS CREDITS

pp.10-11 Ecumenical Program on Central America and the Caribbean

p.14 Puerto Rico Federal Affairs Administration

p.15 (left) Gilberto Hernández, courtesy of the Caribbean Cultural Center, New York City

p.15 (right) Collection of the Museo de Antropología, Historia y Arte, Universidad de Puerto Rico

p.18 Millaray Quiroga, courtesy of the Instituto de Estudios de Población y Desarrollo / PROFAMILIA, Santo Domingo, Dominican Republic

p.23 Néstor Otero

p.27 Néstor Otero

p.31 Néstor Otero

p.32 Néstor Otero

p.35 From *The Art of Rini Templeton: Where There Is Life and Struggle* (Seattle, WA: Real Comet Press and México, D.F., Centro de Documentación Gráfica Rini Templeton)

p.37 Jack Délano, from *Las Caretas de Carton del Carnaval de Ponce* (Ediciones Alba, 1983)

p.38 Library of Congress Collection

p.40 From *Puerto Rican Studies K-Grades 1-2*, Bureau of Curriculum Development, Board of Education of the City of New York

p.43 From *The Art of Rini Templeton*

p.44 From *The Art of Rini Templeton*

pp.48-49 José Rodríguez

p.51 Carlos de Jesús, courtesy of Susan Zeig

p.56 Centro de Estudios Puertorriqueños

p.57 Manuel Otero, courtesy of Centro de Estudios Puertorriqueños, Taller de Migración 1974

p.58 From *Memoirs of Bernardo Vega*

p.61 Schomburg Center for Research in Black Culture

p.63 Schomburg Center for Research in Black Culture

p.69 Centro de Estudios Puertorriqueños

p.71 Manuel Otero, courtesy of Centro de Estudios Puertorriqueños, Taller de Migración 1974

p.72 International Ladies Garment Workers Union

p.74 *Dollars and Sense*

p.78 Catherine A. Sunshine

pp.80-81 From *The Art of Rini Templeton*

p.83 *Claridad*

p.88 PRISA

p.91 Sandra Reus, courtesy of PRISA

p.92 Sandra Reus, courtesy of PRISA

p.95 Néstor Otero

p.97 *San Juan Star*

p.102 Juan Ibáñez, courtesy of *Claridad*

BERMUDA
Hamilton
Col. U.K.
Crown Colony
Pop. 72,000

BAHAMAS
Nassau
Col. U.K.
Ind. 1973
Pop. 241,000

CUBA
Havana
Col. Spain
Ind. 1898
Pop. 9.8 million

CAYMAN ISLANDS
Georgetown
Col. U.K.
Crown Colony
Pop. 20,000

JAMAICA
Kingston
Col. U.K.
Ind. 1962
Pop. 2.2 million

BELIZE
Belmopan
Col. U.K.
Ind. 1981
Pop. 152,000

NETHERLANDS ANTILLES
1. Curaçao
2. Aruba
3. Bonaire
4. St. Maarten
5. Saba
6. St. Eustatius
Willemstad
Col. Holland
Self-governing
    colony
Pop. 260,000

FRENCH GUIANA
Cayenne
Col. France
French overseas
    department
Pop. 77,000

SURINAME
Paramaribo
Col. Holland
Ind. 1975
Pop. 376,000

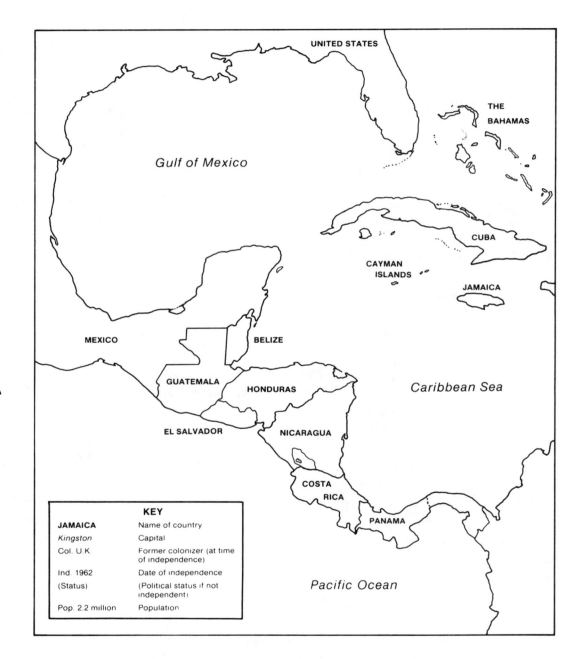

KEY

JAMAICA	Name of country
Kingston	Capital
Col. U.K.	Former colonizer (at time of independence)
Ind. 1962	Date of independence
(Status)	(Political status if not independent)
Pop. 2.2 million	Population

GUYANA
Georgetown
Col. U.K.
Ind. 1966
Pop. 700,000

TRINIDAD AND TOBAGO
Port-of-Spain
Col. U.K.
Ind. 1962
Pop. 1.1 million

GRENADA
St. George's
Col. U.K.
Ind. 1974
Pop. 110,000

BARBADOS
Bridgetown
Col. U.K.
Ind. 1966
Pop. 256,000

ST. VINCENT & THE GRENADINES
Kingstown
Col. U.K.
Ind. 1979
Pop. 123,000

TURKS & CAICOS
Grand Turk
Col. U.K.
Crown Colony
Pop. 8,000

HAITI
Port-au-Prince
Col. France
Ind. 1804
Pop. 5.2 million

DOMINICAN REPUBLIC
Santo Domingo
Col. Spain
Ind. 1844
Pop. 6.3 million

PUERTO RICO
San Juan
Col. Spain/U.S.
U.S. possession
Pop. 3.2 million

BRITISH VIRGIN IS.
Road Town
Col. U.K.
British dependency
Pop. 13,000

U.S. VIRGIN IS.
1. St. Thomas
2. St. Croix
3. St. John
Charlotte Amalie
Col. U.S.
U.S. territory
Pop. 103,000

ANGUILLA
The Valley
Col. U.K.
British dependency
Pop. 7,000

ANTIGUA & BARBUDA
St. John
Col. U.K.
Ind. 1981
Pop. 77,000

ST. KITTS/NEVIS
Basseterre
Col. U.K.
Ind. 1983
Pop. 45,000

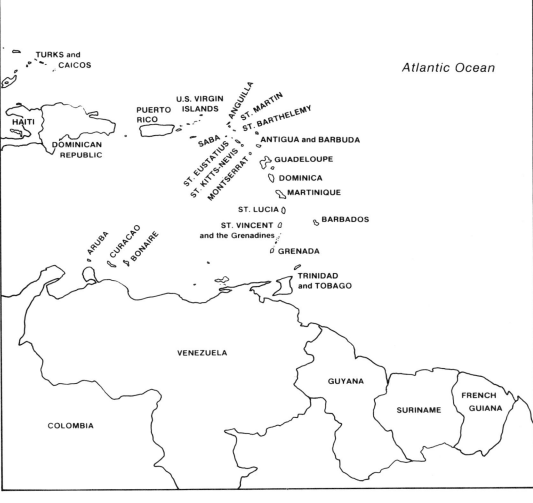

The Caribbean

Atlantic Ocean

ST. LUCIA
Castries
Col. U.K.
Ind. 1979
Pop. 119,000

MARTINIQUE
Fort-de-France
Col. France
French overseas
  department
Pop. 303,000

DOMINICA
Roseau
Col. U.K.
Ind. 1978
Pop. 74,000

GUADELOUPE
Basseterre
Col. France
French overseas
  department
Pop. 328,000

MONTSERRAT
Plymouth
Col. U.K.
Crown Colony
Pop. 12,000

Map Exercises

ACTIVITY 1: FIND THESE COUNTRIES

Instructor: For this exercise, white-out the names of the following countries on the master map. Make a photocopy of the altered map for each student. Break the class into small groups. The groups will use the clues to fill in the names of the missing countries on their maps. They will think of another fact they know about each country and write it in the space provided. (If they do not know, encourage them to guess.) Afterwards, go over each set of clues with the class, asking a student to point out the correct country on a large wall map.

1. **The Dominican Republic** is a Spanish-speaking country. It shares the island of Hispaniola with Haiti.

Something else we know about the Dominican Republic:_____

_____

2. **Barbados** is an English-speaking country. It is the easternmost island in the Caribbean Sea.

Something else we know about Barbados: _____

_____

3. **Trinidad and Tobago** is a twin-island state. It is off the coast of Venezuela at the southern tip of the Caribbean archipelago.

Something else we know about Trinidad and Tobago:_____

_____

4. **Guyana** is an English-speaking country on the South American mainland. It shares a border with Venezuela.

Something else we know about Guyana: _____

_____

5. **Belize** is an English-speaking country located in Central America. It shares borders with Guatemala and Mexico.

Something else we know about Belize: _____

_____

6. **Dominica** is an English-speaking country. It is located between the French territories of Guadeloupe and Martinique.

Something else we know about Dominica: _____

_____

7. **Curaçao** is a Dutch colony. It is off the coast of Venezuela between Aruba and Bonaire.

Something else we know about Curaçao: _____

_____

ACTIVITY 2: WHO AM I?

Instructor: Photocopy the worksheet below for each student. Students will retain their maps from the preceding activity. Break the class into small groups. Each group will fill in the country names on the worksheet and add their own "clues." Afterwards, go over each set of clues with the class, asking a student to point out the correct country on a large wall map.

1. I am an archipelago of many small islands.
I am close to Florida.
My capital is Nassau.

I *am* _____

Our own clue: _____

2. I am south of St. Vincent.
I produce nutmeg.
The United States invaded me in 1983.

I *am* _____

Our own clue: _____

3. I am one of three Spanish-speaking Caribbean nations.
I am near the U.S. Virgin Islands.
I am a United States "Commonwealth."

I *am* _____

Our own clue: _____

4. I am the largest island in the Caribbean.
My capital is Havana.
I produce sugar.

I *am* _____

Our own clue: _____

5. I was colonized by France.
I had a successful slave revolution in 1795.
I share an island with the Dominican Republic.

I *am* _____

Our own clue: _____

6. I am an island south of Cuba.
I produce bauxite.
I am the birthplace of reggae music.

I *am* _____

Our own clue: _____

Puerto Rico at a Glance

Official name: *Estado Libre Asociado de Puerto Rico* (Spanish) – Commonwealth of Puerto Rico (English)

Political status: Territorial possession of the United States

Form of government: The U.S. Congress controls Puerto Rico under Article 4, Section 3 of the U.S. Constitution. Puerto Rico is subject to the juridical/legal system of the United States. U.S. federal government agencies implement federal laws and programs in Puerto Rico. A non-voting Resident Commissioner represents Puerto Rico in the U.S. House of Representatives.

Local government consists of a bicameral Legislative Assembly and a popularly-elected Governor.

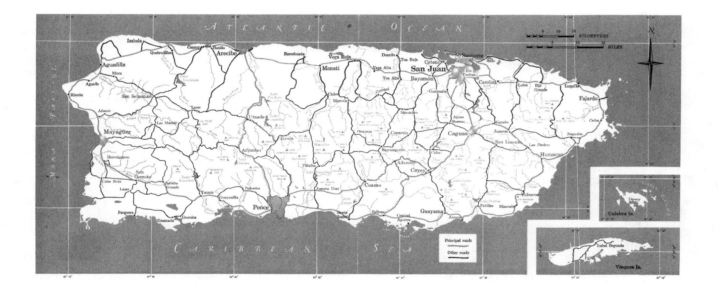

Area: 3,423 square miles

Population: (1986 estimate) 3.3 million in Puerto Rico; 2.6 million in the United States

Capital: San Juan

Second largest city: Ponce

Language: Spanish

Currency: U.S. dollar

A Brief History of Puerto Rico

Long before the Europeans arrived, Puerto Rico was a homeland of the Taíno Arawak. This indigenous people, originally from South America, began migrating northward into the Caribbean as early as 500 B.C.

each governed by a *cacique* or chief. The Arawaks worshipped various deities, and they used carved idols of stone, clay, wood or gold—called *cemís*—to drive away evil spirits and ensure a good harvest.

ment. But the rebellion was crushed, and forced labor and disease greatly reduced the Arawak population.

Those who remained intermarried with the Spanish settlers, producing a people of mixed Spanish-Arawak ancestry. A few settlers owned large coffee and sugar plantations. But most were landless laborers, sharecroppers, or farmers growing just enough food for their own families. These small farmers were called *jíbaros*.

As the Arawak population declined, the Puerto Rican plantation owners turned to African slavery. Although slavery was less extensive in Puerto Rico than in other

Artist's conception of the Arawak supreme deity Yocajú Bagua Morocoti, god of earth, cassava and the sea. Artist: Gilberto Hernández.

They established their main settlements on the islands today known as the Bahamas, Hispaniola, Cuba, Jamaica and Puerto Rico. They called Puerto Rico "Boriquén," or "land of the great lords."

The Arawaks were a peaceful people who lived by farming, hunting and fishing. Corn and cassava were their most important crops. They lived in permanent villages called *yucayeques*,

Christopher Columbus landed on Puerto Rico during his second voyage. In 1508, Juan Ponce de León was sent from the Spanish colony in nearby Santo Domingo to conquer Boriquén for Spain. The Spanish divided up the land among themselves and forced the Arawaks to work in gold mines and on farms and ranches. After three years, the Arawaks revolted against this cruel treat-

An Arawak cemí of carved stone.

Caribbean colonies, African influences enriched Puerto Rican culture. The *bomba* and the *plena* evolved as indigenous Puerto Rican music with roots in West Africa. (*La Bomba and La Plena, Music of Puerto Rico*)

From their Arawak, Spanish and African heritage, Puerto Ricans forged a strong identity as a Spanish-speaking Caribbean people. By the mid-1800s, many people on the island wanted independence from Spanish colonial rule. So did the people of Spain's other Caribbean colony, Cuba; Puerto Ricans and Cubans worked together to plot a struggle

Lola Rodríguez de Tío

against Spain. A Puerto Rican poet and revolutionary, Lola Rodríguez de Tío, wrote:

> Cuba and Puerto Rico are
> the two wings of a bird.
> They receive flowers and bullets
> in the very same heart.

In 1868, a pro-independence insurrection broke out in the town of Lares. *El Grito de Lares* (the Cry of Lares) was led by a Puerto Rican doctor, Ramón Emeterio Betances, from his base in exile. The insurrectionists proclaimed the "First Republic of Puerto Rico," but the Spanish militia crushed the uprising. Afterwards, however, Spain granted some reforms, including the abolition of slavery. At the same time, the colonial authorities forced many pro-independence Puerto Ricans to leave the island; many went into exile in the United States.

The U.S. Takes Over

American business interests, meanwhile, were eager to expand into the Caribbean to profit from fertile land and new markets. They looked for a way to edge Spain out of the region. Rebels in Cuba were already fighting against Spanish rule, and many prominent Americans hoped the United States would enter the war. In 1898 the U.S. battleship Maine exploded in the harbor at Havana, Cuba. The United States seized the moment to declare war on Spain. U.S. Marines invaded Spain's remaining overseas colonies— Cuba, Puerto Rico and the Philippines. When the war was over, a victorious U.S. claimed Puerto Rico as war booty.

Puerto Rico became an "unincorporated territory" of the

Dr. Ramón Emeterio Betances

United States. An American governor took charge of the island. The U.S. Congress controlled Puerto Rico's laws, courts, currency, customs, immigration, defense, foreign relations and trade. English was imposed as the language of instruction in Puerto Rican schools, although neither the students nor most of the teachers could speak it. Puerto Ricans were made U.S. citizens in 1917, eligible to be drafted into the U.S. armed forces. (*A Lead Box That Couldn't Be Opened*)

U.S. corporations moved in and acquired vast tracts of land to set up sugar and tobacco plantations. In the process, many Puerto Rican farmers lost their land and became poorly-paid laborers on the plantations. Others emigrated to Hawaii or Cuba to cut sugar cane. U.S. companies also set up a cottage industry on the island where Puerto Rican women like Minerva Ríos sewed clothes for the U.S. market. (*Memories of Puerto Rico and New York*)

Early Puerto Rican Communities in the U.S.

Puerto Ricans had begun migrating to the United States during the 1800s, when pro-independence nationalists were expelled from the island. Many of the early migrants were *tabaqueros*, or cigar-makers, who came to work in U.S. cigar factories. The *tabaqueros* were skilled artisans who were proud of their trade. They were also among the most educated, well-informed workers, in part because of the tradition in Puerto Rico of having a "reader" read aloud to the workers as they rolled cigars. Cigar-makers like Bernardo Vega helped bring this practice to the United States. (*The Customs and Traditions of the Tabaqueros*)

By the turn of the century, there was a vibrant Puerto Rican community in New York, centered in East Harlem. It had its own social clubs, political organizations and newspapers. But Puerto Ricans also joined U.S. trade unions and political parties, believing that all workers and people of color should struggle together for better conditions. A Black Puerto Rican, Arturo Alfonso Schomburg, became famous as a collector of books on the history of African-Americans. (*Arturo Alfonso Schomburg*)

Operation Bootstrap and Migration to the United States

The Depression of the 1930s worsened the poverty in Puerto Rico. On the island, a movement led by Pedro Albizu Campos and the Nationalist Party demanded independence from the United States. Confrontation between the Nationalists and U.S. federal authorities climaxed in 1937, when police opened fire on a peaceful protest march in Ponce. Eighteen demonstrators were killed and hundreds wounded in the "Ponce Massacre."

While forcibly suppressing the pro-independence movement, U.S. officials also sought to reduce its appeal by improving conditions on the island. Working with a new Puerto Rican leader, Luis Muñoz Marín, the U.S. gave the island more internal self-government. In 1948, for the first time, Puerto Ricans elected their own governor. In 1952 a new constitution defined Puerto Rico as a "Free Associated State" voluntarily linked to the U.S. But the U.S. Congress remained in charge of the most important laws and decisions affecting the island.

The reforms included a plan to reduce poverty by attracting industry to Puerto Rico. Under "Operation Bootstrap," Congress offered U.S. corporations special tax breaks to open factories on the island. U.S. and Puerto Rican planners hoped these factories would relieve unemployment. But they had another goal as well: to provide cheap labor for U.S. industry. Factory workers in Puerto Rico earned on average 40 cents an hour in 1950, compared to $1.50 an hour

Pedro Albizu Campos

for U.S. workers. In the early 1960s, firms making shoes, clothing and glassware opened factories in Puerto Rico to take advantage of tax exemptions and low wages.

But the factories could not

Artist: Millaray Quiroga

and early 1960s. U.S. capital investment soared from $1.4 billion in 1960 to $24 billion in 1979. The island's middle class expanded, and many people acquired consumer goods like cars and televisions.

By middle of the 1960s, however, many of the foreign firms had closed their Puerto Rican plants. Cheaper wages could be had elsewhere, in nearby Haiti or in the Far East. Unemployment began rising again. Over the last decade it has fluctuated between 15 and 23 percent, according to official figures. It would be still higher if many Puerto Ricans did not migrate to the United States to seek work there.

In the rush to industrialize, Puerto Rico stopped growing its own food. Today, 85 percent of what Puerto Ricans eat is imported—mostly from the United States—and is sold on the island for jacked-up prices. To keep living standards up, the U.S. government provides an array of welfare benefits to many Puerto Rican households. These benefits, called "transfer payments," account for 30 percent of all personal income in Puerto Rico.

In the late 1960s a new type of industry came to Puerto Rico. These were giant petroleum refining, petrochemical and pharmaceutical firms, such as Du Pont, Union Carbide and Gulf Oil. These highly mechanized industries created few jobs for Puerto Ricans; instead, companies often brought in skilled workers and technicians from the United States. But

employ all the people who had lost their land or jobs in agriculture. So as part of the Bootstrap plan, U.S. and Puerto Rican authorities organized a huge migration of Puerto Ricans to the United States. U.S. steel manufacturers, auto makers and garment firms sent delegations to the island to recruit workers. Between 1945 and 1965, over half a million Puerto Ricans migrated.

They settled mostly in east coast and midwest cities like New York, Philadelphia and

Chicago. Industries in these cities, especially New York's clothing manufacturers, depended on Puerto Rican labor. Younger Puerto Ricans born in the United States recall their parents' years of factory labor with both pride and sadness. (*Our Mothers' Struggle Has Shown Us the Way*)

Puerto Rico Today

Operation Bootstrap was touted as an economic miracle, and for a while, it appeared to be. The Puerto Rican economy grew rapidly during the 1950s they produced huge amounts of toxic waste, polluting air and water all over the island.

Puerto Ricans living near the industries have experienced abnormal rates of illness such as cancer and respiratory ailments. Around the island, community groups have demanded that government and company officials respond to the pollution problem. A few efforts have been successful, but most have met with frustration. (*Operation Bootstrap's Legacy*)

Another controversial issue is militarism. As the major United States military base in the Caribbean, Puerto Rico houses a vast complex of U.S. military facilities, including the Roosevelt Roads Naval Station, the Ramey Air Force Base, and the Salinas National Guard Camp. All these areas are off-limits to Puerto Ricans. The Navy uses the small offshore island of Vieques for training and target practice. (*Vieques and the Navy*) Members of the Puerto Rican National Guard, which is part of the U.S. National Guard, have been sent to Central America to take part in military exercises.

These problems—unemployment, industrial pollution, and militarism—have made many people aware that Puerto Rico's special relationship with the U.S. has costs as well as benefits. Many Puerto Ricans believe that the island's relationship to the United States is actually a colonial one. But there is no agreement on whether to change it, or on what its replacement should be.

The main alternatives to the present arrangement are statehood and independence. Should Puerto Rico become a new U.S. state, like Hawaii and Alaska? Or should it become an independent country, on its own, and in charge of its own destiny?

Whatever opinions Puerto Ricans may hold, it is still the U.S. Congress—not Puerto Rico—which has the legal power to determine the island's political status. But pressure for change is growing, and there is talk of a plebiscite in which Puerto Ricans could vote their preference among the three alternatives: statehood, independence, or continued Commonwealth. Before this can happen, U.S. and Puerto Rican officials need to agree on what each option would mean for a range of issues, from the taxes Puerto Ricans pay to the languages they speak. (*What Future for Puerto Rico?*) Within the limited range of options acceptable to Washington, Puerto Ricans may finally be given the opportunity to decide what future of their homeland will be.

Further Reading on Puerto Rican History

Ricardo E. Alegría, *History of the Indians of Puerto Rico* (San Juan, 1970).

Salvador Brau, *Historia de Puerto Rico* (San Juan: Editorial Coquí, 1966; first published 1904).

Raymond Carr, *Puerto Rico: A Colonial Experiment* (New York Univrsity Press, 1984).

Eugenio Fernández Méndez, *Art and Mythology of the Taíno Indians of the Greater West Indies* (San Juan, 1972).

Loida Figueroa, *History of Puerto Rico* (Anaya Book Co., 1972).

Adalberto López, *The Puerto Ricans: Their History, Culture and Society* (Schenkman Pub. Co., 1980).

Loretta Phelps de Córdova, *Five Centuries in Puerto Rico: Portraits and Eras* (Inter American University Press, 1988).

Juan Angel Sílen, *We the Puerto Rican People* (Modern Reader, 1971).

Kal Wagenheim, *Puerto Rico: A Profile* (Praeger Books, 1970).

Important Dates in Puerto Rican History

pre-1493
Island is a homeland of the Arawaks, a native people originally from South America. They call it "Boriquén."

1493
Christopher Columbus lands on the island and claims it for Spain.

1511
Arawak revolt against Spanish occupation.

1520s
Beginning use of Africans as slave labor.

1822
Slave uprising.

1865
Cuban and Puerto Rican emigrants in New York City form Republican Society to agitate for independence from Spain.

1868
Lares Rebellion, demanding Puerto Rico's independence from Spain.

1873
Slavery abolished in Puerto Rico.

1898
U.S. troops invade Puerto Rico during Spanish-American War. Spain cedes Puerto Rico to the U.S. under Treaty of Paris.

1898-1900
U.S. military governs Puerto Rico.

1900
U.S. Congress passes Foraker Act, establishing a U.S.-controlled civilian government.

1917
Puerto Ricans made U.S. citizens.

1922
Nationalist Party founded, demanding Puerto Rico's independence from the U.S.

1929
Depression hits Puerto Rico.

1937
Police open fire on peaceful protest march by the Nationalist Party in the city of Ponce, killing 18 people.

1938
Luis Muñoz Marín founds the Popular Democratic Party.

1946
Puerto Rican Independence Party founded.

1947
Beginning of "Operation Bootstrap" industrialization plan and mass emigration to the United States.

1948
Muñoz Marín becomes first elected governor of Puerto Rico.

1950
Nationalist uprising. Thousands of independence sympathizers are jailed.

1952
"Commonwealth" status implemented.

1967
New Progressive Party founded, advocating U.S. statehood for Puerto Rico.

1972
Decolonization committee of the United Nations declares Puerto Rico to be a colony of the United States and demands self-determination for the island.

1975
Official unemployment rate reaches 20 percent.

1987
Puerto Rican population living in the U.S. reaches two and a half million.

1989
Governor of Puerto Rico asks U.S. Congress for a plebiscite on the island's future status.

TEACHER GUIDE
A Lead Box That Couldn't Be Opened

▶ **OBJECTIVES**

Students will:

1. List and evaluate some characteristics of Puerto Rican community life

2. Speculate on the author's purpose in writing the story

3. Draw preliminary conclusions concerning the relationship of Puerto Rico to the United States

▶ **QUESTIONS FOR DISCUSSION**

1. When did the story take place, approximately? What do you know about the Korean War?

2. Was Puerto Rico at war with Korea? Why was Moncho Ramírez fighting there? What questions does this raise for you, that you may need more information to answer?

3. Describe the relationship between the neighbors who lived in the *ranchón*. How did they react to a crisis? How did the author feel about this? How do you think the lieutenant may have felt?

4. Has any member of your family served in the U.S. military? How did you feel about it? Now, imagine you or a family member were drafted to serve in the armed forces of another country, not the United States. Would this be possible? How would you feel?

▶ **SUGGESTED ACTIVITIES**

1. The class stages a skit based on the story.

2. Students research the subject of Puerto Ricans in the U.S. military (including the National Guard). How many have served? What wars have they fought in? What percentage of the U.S. armed forces is currently made up of Puerto Ricans? What role have Puerto Ricans played in the conflicts in Central America? Possible sources include:

  • Puerto Rico Federal Affairs Administration, 734 15th St., NW, Suite 700, Washington, DC 20005

  • Veteran's Administration, Public Relations Office, 810 Vermont Ave., N.W., Washington, DC 20420.

  • Caribbean Project for Justice & Peace, P.O. Box 21226, Río Piedras, PR 00928.

▶ **RESOURCES**

1. Three anthologies of short stories by Puerto Rican writers:

  • Kal Wagenheim, ed., *Cuentos: An Anthology of Short Stories from Puerto Rico* (Schocken Books, 1978). Bilingual, with Spanish and English text on facing pages.

• María Teresa Babín and Stan Steiner, eds., *Borinquen: An Anthology of Puerto Rican Literature* (Vintage Books, 1974). Short stories, poems and songs in English translation.

• Robert L. Muckley and Eduardo E. Vargas, eds., *Cuentos Puertorriqueños* (National Textbook Co., 1988). Nine stories in Spanish, including the original of José Luis González's *Una caja de plomo que no se podía abrir*. With glossary and discussion questions. Available from National Textbook Co., 4255 West Touhy Ave., Lincolnwood, IL 60646.

INTRODUCTION
A Lead Box That Couldn't Be Opened

When Puerto Ricans were made U.S. citizens in 1917, they became eligible to be drafted into the U.S. armed forces. Military recruitment was active on the island, as it still is today. Thousands of Puerto Ricans fought for the United States in World Wars One and Two, in the Korean War, and in Vietnam.

José Luis González is one of Puerto Rico's best-known writers of fiction. His short story, *Una caja de plomo que no se podía abrir* (A Lead Box That Couldn't Be Opened), dramatizes the impact on a working-class Puerto Rican community when "the war comes home."

About the artist:
Puerto Rico-born Néstor Otero is a visual artist who lives and works in New York City. He is a Vietnam veteran.

Artist: Néstor Otero

READING

A Lead Box That Couldn't Be Opened

BY JOSÉ LUIS GONZÁLEZ

This happened two years ago, when they brought back the remains of Moncho⁰ Ramírez, who died in Korea. Well now, this business about "the remains of Moncho Ramírez" is a figure of speech, because nobody ever found out what was really inside that lead box that couldn't be opened; and that was what drove Doña Milla⁰, Moncho's mother, nearly out of her head, because she wanted to see her son before they buried him. But it would be better to start the story from the beginning.

Six months after they sent Moncho Ramírez to Korea, Doña Milla received a letter from the government saying that Moncho was on the list of those missing in action. Doña Milla had a neighbor read the letter to her because it came from the United States and was written in English. When Doña Milla found out what the letter said she locked herself in her two rooms and spent three days weeping. She wouldn't open the door for anyone, not even the neighbors who came to bring her *guarapillos*⁰.

There was a lot of talk in the *ranchón*⁰ about the disappearance of Moncho Ramírez. At the beginning, some of us thought that surely Moncho had gotten lost in some forest and would reappear one day. Others said that at best, the Koreans had

taken him prisoner and would release him after the war was over. In the evenings after supper, we men would gather on the porch of the *ranchón* and discuss these two possibilities, so that we began referring to ourselves as "the lost ones" and "the prisoners" according to which theory we supported. Now that it's all just a memory, I ask myself how many of us thought, without saying it, that Moncho was neither lost in a forest nor a war prisoner, but was actually dead. I thought it many times, but never said anything, and it seems to me now that it was like that for everyone. Because it's not good to give someone up for dead— much less a close friend like Moncho Ramírez, who was born in that very *ranchón*, before you know for sure. Besides, how were we going to have our evening discussions on the porch if there weren't different opinions?

Two months after that first letter, another arrived. This second letter, which the neighbor also read to Doña Milla because it was in English like the first, said that Moncho Ramírez had appeared. Or rather, what was left of Moncho Ramírez. We learned this from the screams that Doña Milla let out as soon as she realized what the letter said. That afternoon the whole *ranchón* crowded into

Doña Milla's two rooms. I don't know how we managed to fit but every one of us was there, and we were quite a few. The women had to put Doña Milla to bed, even though it wasn't night, because she was driving herself nearly crazy with screaming, looking at the portrait of Moncho in his military uniform posed between an American flag and an eagle with a bunch of arrows in its talons. We men drifted out to the porch little by little, but that night there was no discussion because we all knew Moncho was dead and it was impossible to imagine anything else.

Three months later they brought the lead box that couldn't be opened. Four soldiers of the Military Police armed with rifles and wearing white gloves brought it in an Army truck, with no notice beforehand. The four soldiers were commanded by a lieutenant who didn't carry a rifle but had a .45 in his belt. He got out of the truck first. He paused in the middle of the street, hands on hips and legs apart, looking at the facade of the *ranchón* the way one man looks at another when he's about to ask for an explanation for some offense. Afterwards he turned his head and said to those in the truck: "Yes, it's here. Come on." The four soldiers got out of the truck, two of them carrying the box, which wasn't the size of a coffin but smaller, and which was covered with an American flag.

The lieutenant had to ask a group of neighbors standing on the sidewalk which was the room of the Ramírez widow. (You know how these *ranchones* are in Puerta de Tierra[0]: fifteen or twenty doors, each of them to one dwelling; and most of them without a number or anything to indicate who lives there.) The neighbors not only informed the lieutenant that Doña Milla's door was the fourth one to the left, but also followed the five soldiers into the *ranchón* without taking their eyes off that box covered with the American flag. The lieutenant, visibly bothered by this accompaniment, knocked on the door with a white-gloved hand. Doña Milla opened the door and the officer asked her:

"Are you Señora Emilia[0], widow of Ramírez?"[0]

Doña Milla did not answer right away. She looked first at the lieutenant, then at the four soldiers, at the neighbors, and at the box.

"Ah?" she said, as if she hadn't heard the officer's question.

"*Señora*, you are Doña Emilia, widow of Ramírez?"

Doña Milla looked again at the box covered with the flag. She lifted a hand, pointed, and asked in a faint voice:

"What is that?"

The lieutenant replied with a touch of impatience:

"*Señora*, you are ..."

"What is that, ah?" Doña Milla asked again, in that tremulous tone of voice with which women always anticipate the confirmation of a disaster. "Tell me! What is it?"

The lieutenant turned and looked at the neighbors. He read in each pair of eyes the same question. He turned back to the woman, cleared his throat, and said finally:

"*Señora* ..." he began again. "Your son, Corporal Ramón Ramírez ..."

After these words he said others, but no one heard them because Doña Milla had already begun to emit screams, tremendous screams which seemed like they would tear her throat apart.

What happened then was so confused that I, standing in the group of neighbors behind the soldiers, cannot remember it precisely. Someone gave a strong push and within a few seconds we were all inside Doña Milla's rooms. A woman shouted for *agua de azahar*[0] while trying to prevent Doña Milla from clawing her face with her fingernails. The lieutenant began saying "Calm! Calm!" but no one paid any attention to him. Neighbors kept arriving, drawn by the tumult, until it was impossible to move inside the apartment. Several women finally managed to take Doña Milla into the bedroom. They had her drink *agua de azahar* and put her to bed. We men were left alone in the outer room. The lieutenant addressed us with a forced smile:

"Well, boys ... You were

friends of Corporal Ramírez, isn't that so?"

No one answered. The lieutenant went on:

"Well, boys ... Since the women are calming down, you can help me, right? Put that little table in the middle of the room for me. We'll put the box there to watch over it."

One of us spoke for the first time. It was old Sotero Valle, who had worked on the docks with the late Artemio Ramírez, Doña Milla's husband. He pointed to the box covered with the American flag and asked the lieutenant:

"In there ... in there ...?"

"Yes sir," said the lieutenant. "That box contains the remains of Corporal Ramírez. You knew Corporal Ramírez?"

"He was my godson," answered Sotero Valle, very quietly, as if afraid he wouldn't be able to finish the sentence.

"Corporal Ramírez died fulfilling his duty," said the lieutenant, and no one spoke again.

This was around 5 o'clock in the afternoon. That evening, the people couldn't even fit into the apartment: they came from all over the neighborhood, filled the porch and spilled out onto the sidewalk. Those of us inside drank coffee which a neighbor woman brought from time to time. People brought chairs from other apartments, but most of those present remained standing; we took up less space that way. The women remained closed in the bedroom with

Doña Milla. One of them would come out every so often to ask for something—water, alcohol, coffee—and would tell us:

"She's calmer now. I think she'll be able to come out in a short while."

The four soldiers kept guard, rifles on their shoulders, two on each side of the little table which held the box covered with the flag. The lieutenant had posted himself at the foot of the table, with his back to the table and the four soldiers, his feet slightly apart and hands behind his back. When the coffee first arrived, someone offered him a cup, but he didn't accept. He said he could not interrupt the watch.

Old Sotero wasn't drinking coffee either. He had seated himself at the beginning facing the table and had spoken to no one during the whole time. And during the whole time he hadn't stopped staring at the box. His gaze was strange: he seemed to look without seeing. Suddenly, as they were serving coffee for the fourth time, he got up from the chair and placed himself in front of the lieutenant.

"Look," he said without looking at him, his eyes still fixed on the box. "You say my godson Ramón Ramírez is in this box?"

"Yes sir," answered the officer.

"But ... but ... in such a small box?"

The lieutenant explained, with some difficulty:

"Well ... look ... these are just the remains of Corporal Ramírez."

"You mean ... that's all they found ..."

"Only the remains, yes sir. Undoubtedly he had been dead for some time. That happens in war, see?"

The old man said nothing more. Still standing, he looked a few moments more at the box; then returned to his seat.

A few minutes later the door of the bedroom opened and Doña Milla came out, supported on the arms of two women. She was pale and disheveled, but her face reflected a great serenity. She walked slowly, still supported by the two women, until she came face to face with the lieutenant and said to him: "Señor° ... please be so kind as to ... tell us how to open the box."

The lieutenant looked at her surprised.

"Señora, this box can't be opened. It's sealed."

Doña Milla seemed not to understand right away. She widened her eyes and stared at the officer, until he felt constrained to repeat:

"The box is sealed, señora. It can't be opened."

The woman slowly shook her head from side to side. "But I want to see my son. I want to see my son, do you understand? I can't let him be buried without seeing him for the last time."

The lieutenant looked then at us; his look pleaded for understanding, but nobody said a word. Doña Milla took a step toward the box, delicately pulled back a corner of the flag, and tapped lightly.

"Señor" she said to the officer, without looking at him, "this box isn't made of wood. What is it made of, señor?"

"It's lead, señora. They make them like that to withstand the sea voyage from Korea."

"Lead?" murmured Doña Milla without taking her eyes off the box. "And it can't be opened?"

The lieutenant, looking at us again, repeated, "They make them like that to withstand the sea voy—"

But he couldn't finish; he was interrupted by the terrible screams of Doña Milla, screams which made me feel as though someone had suddenly punched me in the stomach:

"MONCHO! MONCHO, MY SON, NOBODY IS GOING TO BURY YOU WITHOUT ME SEEING YOU! NOBODY, MY SON, NOBODY ...!"

Once again it's difficult for me to say exactly what happened: Doña Milla's cries produced great confusion. The two women who supported her tried to get her away from the box, but she frustrated their efforts by going limp and collapsing on the floor. Some of the men stepped forward to intervene. I didn't; I was already feeling that sensation in the pit of my stomach. Old Sotero was one of those who went to help Doña Emilia, and I sat down in his chair. No, I'm not ashamed to say it, I either had to sit down or else leave the room. I don't know if such a thing has ever

Artist: Néstor Otero

happened to you. It wasn't fear, because there was no danger to me at that moment. But my stomach was clenched hard like a fist, and my legs felt as if suddenly they had turned into jelly. If that has ever happened to one of you, you'll know what I mean. If not ... well, if not, I hope it never does. Or at least that it happens where no one can see you.

I sat down. I sat down and, in the midst of the terrible confusion that surrounded me, thought about Moncho as I had never in my life thought about him before. Doña Milla had cried herself hoarse, as they led her slowly toward the bedroom, and I thought about Moncho, about Moncho who was born in this same *ranchón* where I was born, about Moncho who was the only one not to cry when they took us to school for the first time, about Moncho who swam farther than anyone when we went to the beach behind the Capitolio°, about Moncho who had always been fourth batter when we played baseball on Isla Grande°, before they built the air base there ... Doña Milla continued crying that they couldn't bury her son until she had seen him for the last time. But the box was made of lead and couldn't be opened.

They buried Moncho Ramírez the next day. A detachment of soldiers fired in the air when the remains of Moncho—or whatever it was inside the box—descended into the deep, damp hole that was his tomb. Doña Milla kneeled on the ground throughout the ceremony.

All this happened two years ago. It didn't occur to me to tell the story until now. Most likely someone will ask why. I will say that this morning the letter-carrier came to the *ranchón*. I didn't have to ask anyone's help to read what he brought me, because I know my little bit of English. It was my notice to report for military service.

–José Luis González, *Una caja de plomo que no se podía abrir*, translated and reprinted by permission of the author. Translation by C. Sunshine.

Vocabulary

Moncho: nickname for Ramón

Doña: title of respect for a married or older woman

guarapillo: a hot drink, like herb tea

ranchón: long, low building resembling a barracks, with a number of apartments side by side

Puerta de Tierra: working-class section of San Juan

señora: Madam or Mrs.

widow of Ramírez: In Spanish-speaking countries, after a woman's husband dies, she uses "widow of" (*viuda de*) with his last name.

agua de azahar: drink made from flowers of the orange or lemon tree

señor: Sir or Mr.

Capitolio: the Capitol building in San Juan where the Puerto Rican assembly meets

Isla Grande: an area of San Juan

READING
Una caja de plomo que no se podía abrir

POR JOSÉ LUIS GONZÁLEZ

Esto sucedio hace dos años, cuando llegaron los restos de Moncho Ramírez, que murió en Corea. Bueno, eso de "los restos de Moncho Ramírez" es un decir, porque la verdad es que nadie llegó a saber nunca lo que había dentro de aquella caja de plomo que no se podía abrir. De plomo, sí señor, y que no se podía abrir; y eso fue lo que puso como loca a doña Milla, la mamá de Moncho, porque lo que ella quería era ver a su hijo antes de lo enterraran. Pero más vale que yo empiece a contar esto desde el principio.

Seis meses después que se llevaron a Moncho Ramírez a Corea, doña Milla, recibió una carta del gobierno que decía que Moncho estaba en la lista de los desaparecidos en combate. La carta se la dio doña Milla a un vecino para que se la leyera porque venía de los Estados Unidos y estaba en inglés. Cuando doña Milla se enteró de lo que decía la carta se encerró en sus dos piezas y se pasó tres días llorando. No les abrió la puerta ni a las vecinas que fueron a llevarle guarapillos.

En el ranchón se habló muchísimo de la desaparición de Moncho Ramírez. Al principio algunos opinamos que Moncho seguramente se había perdido en algún monte y que ya aparecería cualquier día. Otros dijeron que a lo mejor los coreanos lo habían hecho prisionero y después de la guerra lo devolverían. Por las noches, después de comer, los hombres nos reuníamos en el patio del ranchón y nos poníamos a discutir sobre esas dos posibilidades, y así vinimos a llamarnos "los perdidos" y "los prisioneros," según lo que pensáramos que le había sucedido a Moncho Ramírez. Ahora que ya todo eso es un recuerdo, yo me pregunto cuántos de nosotros pensábamos, sin decirlo, que Moncho no estaba perdido en ningún monte ni era prisionero de los coreanos, sino que estaba muerto. Yo pensaba eso muchas veces pero nunca lo decía, y ahora me parece que a todos les pasaba igual. Porque no está bien eso de ponerse a dar por muerto a nadie—y menos a un buen amigo como era Moncho Ramírez, que había nacido en el ranchón—antes de saberlo uno con seguridad. Y, además, ¿cómo íbamos a discutir por las noches en el patio del ranchón si no había dos opiniones diferentes?

Dos meses después de la primera carta, llegó otra. Esta segunda carta, que le leyó a doña Milla el mismo vecino porque estaba en inglés igual que la primera, decía que Moncho Ramírez había aparecido. O, mejor dicho, lo que quedaba de Moncho Ramírez. Nosotros nos enteramos de eso por los gritos que empezó a dar doña Milla tan pronto supo lo que decía la carta. Aquella tarde todo de ranchón se vació en las dos piezas de doña Milla. Yo no sé cómo cabíamos allí pero allí estábamos toditos, y éramos unos cuantos como quien dice. A doña Milla tuvieron que acostarla las mujeres cuando todovía no era de noche porque de tanto gritar, mirando el retrato de Moncho en uniforme militar entre una bandera americana y un águila con un mazo de flechas entre las garras, se había puesto como tonta. Los hombres nos fuimos saliendo al patio poco a poco, pero aquella noche no hubo discusión porque ya todos sabíamos que Moncho estaba muerto y era imposible ponerse a imaginar.

Tres meses después llegó la caja de plomo que no se podía abrir. La trajeron una tarde, sin avisar, en un camión del Ejército, cuatro soldados de la Policía Militar armados de rifles y con guantes blancos. A los cuatro soldados los mandaba un teniente, que no traía rifle pero sí una cuarenticinco en la cintura. Ese fue el primero en bajar del camión. Se paró en el medio de la calle, con los puños en las caderas y las piernas abiertas y miró la fachada del ranchón como mira un hombre a otro cuando va a pedirle cuentas por alguna ofensa. Después volteó la cabeza y les dijo a los que estaban en el camión: "Sí, aquí es. Bájense." Los cuatro soldados se apearon, dos de ellos cargando la caja, que no era del tamaño de un ataúd sino más pequeña y estaba cubierta con una bandera americana.

El teniente tuvo que preguntar, a un grupo de vecinos en la acera cuál era la pieza de la viuda de Ramírez (ustedes saben cómo son ranchones de Puerta de Tierra: quince o viente puertas, cada una de las cuales da a una vivienda, y la mayoría de las puertas sin número ni nada que indique quién vive allí.) Los vecinos no sólo le informaron al teniente que la puerta de doña Milla era la cuarta a mano izquierda entrando, sino que siguieron a los cinco militares dentro del ranchón sin despegar los ojos de la caja cubierta con la bandera americana. El teniente, visiblemente molesto por el acompañamiento, tocó a la puerta con la mano enguantada de blanco. Abrió doña Milla y el oficial le preguntó:

"¿La señora Emilia viuda de Ramírez?"

Doña Milla no contestó en seguida. Miró sucesivamente al teniente, a los cuatro soldados, a los vecinos, a la caja.

"¿Ah?" dijo como si no hubiera oído la pregunta del oficial.

"Señora, ¿usted es doña Emilia viuda de Ramírez?"

Doña Milla volvió a mirar la caja cubierta con la bandera. Levantó una mano, señaló, preguntó con la voz delgadita:

"¿Qué es eso?"

El teniente repitió, con un dejo de impaciencia:

"Señora, ¿usted es ..."

"¿Qué es eso, ah?" preguntó otra vez doña Milla, en ese trémulo tono de voz con que una mujer se anticipa siempre a la confirmación de una desgracia. "¡Dígame! ¿Qué es eso?"

El teniente volteó la cabeza, miró a los vecinos. Leyó en los ojos de todos la misma interrogación. Se volvió nuevamente hacia la mujer; carraspeó; dijo al fin:

"Señora ... El Ejército de los Estados Unidos ..."

Se interrumpió, como quien olvida de repente algo que está acostumbrado a decir de memoria.

"Señora ..." recomenzó. "Su hijo, el cabo Ramón Ramírez ..."

Después de esas palabras dijo otras, que nadie llegó a escuchar porque ya doña Milla había puesto a dar gritos, unos gritos tremendos que parecían desgarrarle la garganta.

Lo que sucedió inmediatamente después resultó demasiado confuso para que yo, que estaba en el grupo de vecinos detrás de los militares, pueda recordarle bien. Alguien empujó con fuerza y en unos instantes todos nos encontramos dentro la pieza de doña Milla. Una mujer pidió agua de azahar a voces,

mientras trataba de impedir que doña Milla se clavara las uñas en el rostro. El teniente empezó a decir: "¡Calma! ¡Calma!" pero nadie le hizo caso. Más y más vecinos fueron llegando, convocados por el tumulto, hasta que resultó imposible dar un paso dentro de la pieza. Al fin varias mujeres lograron llevarse a doña Milla a la otra habitación. La hicieron tomar el agua de azahar y la acostaron en la cama. En la primera pieza quedamos sólo los hombres. El teniente se dirigió entonces a nosotros con una sonrisa forzada: "Bueno, muchachos ... Ustedes eran amigos del cabo Ramírez, ¿verdad?"

Nadie contestó. El teniente añadió:

"Bueno, muchachos ... en lo que las mujeres se calman, ustedes pueden ayudarme, ¿no? Pónganme aquella mesita en el medio de la pieza. Vamos a colocar la caja ahí para hacerle la guardia."

Uno de nosotros habló entonces por primera vez. Fue el viejo Sotero Valle, que había sido compañero de trabajo en los muelles del difunto Artemio Ramírez, esposo de doña Milla. Señaló la caja cubierta con la bandera americana y empezó a interrogar al teniente:

"¿Ahí ... ahí ...?"

"Sí, señor," dijo el teniente, "esa caja contiene los restos del cabo Ramírez. ¿Usted conocía al cabo Ramírez?"

"Era mi ajihado," contestó Sotero Valle, muy quedo, como si temiera no llegar a concluir la frase.

"El cabo Ramírez murió en el cumplimiento de su deber," dijo el teniente, y ya nadie volvió a hablar.

Eso fue como a las cinco de la tarde. Por la noche no cabía la gente en la pieza: habían llegado vecinos de todo el barrio, que llenaban el patio y llegaban hasta la acera. Adentro tomábamos el café que colaba de hora en hora una vecina. De otras piezas se habían traído varias sillas, pero lo más de los presentes estábamos de pie; así ocupábamos menos espacio. Las mujeres seguían encerradas con doña Milla en la otra habitación. Una de ellas salía de vez en cuando a buscar cualquier cosa—agua, alcoholado, café—y aprovechaba para informarnos:

"Ya está bastante calmada. Yo creo que de aquí a un rato podrá salir."

Los cuatro soldados montaban guardia, rifle al hombro, dos a cada lado de la mesita sobre la que descansaba la caja cubierta con la bandera. El teniente se había apostado al pie de la mesita, de espaldas a ésta y a sus cuatro hombres, las piernas un poco separadas y las manos a la espalda. Al principio, cuando se coló el primer café, alguien le ofreció una taza, pero él no la aceptó. Dijo que no se podía interrumpir la guardia.

El viejo Sotero tampoco quiso tomar café. Se había sentado desde un principio frente a la mesita y no le había dirigido la palabra a nadie

durante todo ese tiempo. Y durante todo ese tiempo no había despegado la mirada de la caja. Era una mirada rara la del viejo Sotero: parecía que miraba sin ver. De repente (en los momentos en que servían café por cuarta vez) se levantó de la silla y se le paró por delante al teniente.

Artist: *Néstor Otero*

"Oiga," le dijo, sin mirarlo, fijos siempre los ojos en la caja. "¿Dice usté que en esa caja está mi ajihado Ramón Ramírez?"

"Sí, señor," contestó el oficial.

"Pero ... pero, ¿en esa caja tan chiquita?"

El teniente explicó entonces, con alguna dificultad:

"Bueno ... mire ... es que ahí sólo están los restos del cabo Ramírez."

"¿Quiere decir que ... que lo único que encontraron ..."

"Solamente los restos, sí señor. Seguramente ya había muerto hacía bastante tiempo. Así sucede en la guerra, ¿ve?"

El viejo no dijo nada más. Todovía de pie, miró la caja un

rato; después volvió a su silla.

Unos minutos más tarde se abrió la puerta de la otra habitación y doña Milla salió apoyada en los brazos de dos vecinas. Estaba pálida y despeinada, pero su semblante reflejaba una gran serenidad. Caminó lentamente, siempre apoyada en las otras dos mujeres, hasta llegar frente al teniente. Le dijo:

"Señor ... tenga la bondad ... díganos cómo se abre la caja."

El teniente la miró un poco sorprendido.

"Señora, la caja no se puede abrir. Está sellada."

Doña Milla pareció no conmprender de momento. Agrandó los ojos y los fijó largamente en los del oficial, hasta que éste se sintió obligado a repetir:

"La caja está sellada, señora. No se puede abrir."

La mujer movió de un lado a otro, lentamente, la cabeza:

"Pero yo quiero ver a mi hijo. Yo quiero ver a mi hijo, ¿usted

Artist: Néstor Otero

me entiende? Yo no puedo dejar que lo entierren sin verlo por última vez."

El teniente nos miró entonces a nosotros; era evidente que su mirada solicitaba comprensión, pero nadie dijo una palabra. Doña Milla dio un paso hacia la caja, retiró con delicadeza una punta de la bandera, tocó levemente.

"Señor," le dijo al oficial, sin mirarlo, "esta caja no es de madera. ¿De qué es esta caja, señor?"

"Es de plomo, señora. Las hacen así para que resistan mejor el viaje por mar desde Corea."

"¿De plomo?" murmuró doña Milla sin apartar la mirada de la caja. "¿Y no se puede abrir?"

El teniente, mirándonos nuevamente a nosotros, repetió:

"Las hacen así para que resistan mejor la via ..."

Pero no pudo terminar; no lo dejaron terminar los gritos terribles de doña Milla, unos gritos que a mí me hicieron sentir como si repentinamente me hubieran golpeado en la boca del estómago:

"¡MONCHO! ¡MONCHO, HIJO MIO, NADIE VA A ENTERRARTE SIN QUE YO TE VEA! ¡NADIE, HIJO MIO, NADIE ...!"

Otra vez se me hace difícil contar con exactitud: los gritos de doña Milla produjeron una gran confusión. Las dos mujeres que la sostenían por los brazos trataron de alejarla de la caja, pero ella frustró el intento aflojando el cuerpo y dejándose ir hacia el suelo. Entonces intervinieron varios hombres. Yo no: yo todavía experimentaba aquella sensación en la boca del estómago. El viejo Sotero fue uno de los que acudieron junto a doña Emilia, y yo me senté en su silla. No, no me da vergüenza decirlo: o me sentaba o tenía que salir de la pieza. Yo no sé si a alguno de ustedes le ha sucedido eso alguna vez. Y eso no es miedo, porque ningún peligro me amenazaba en aquel momento. Pero yo sentía el estómago apretado y duro como un puño, y las piernas como si súbitamente se me hubiesen vuelto de trapo. Si a alguno de ustedes le ha sucedido eso alguna vez, sabrá lo que quiero decir. Si no ... bueno, si no, ojalá que no le suceda nunca. O por lo menos que le suceda donde la gente no se dé cuenta.

Yo me senté. Me senté y, en medio de la terrible confusión que me rodeaba, me puse a pensar en Moncho como nunca en mi vida había pensado en él. Doña Milla gritaba hasta enronquecer mientras la iban arrastrando lentamente hacia la otra habitación, y yo pensaba en Moncho, en Moncho que nació en aquel mismo ranchón donde también nací yo, en Moncho que fue el único que no lloró cuando nos llevaron a la escuela por primera vez, en Moncho que nadaba más lejos que nadie cuando íbamos a la playa detrás de Capitolio, en Moncho que había sido siempre cuarto bate cuando jugábamos pelota en Isla Grande, antes de que

hicieran allí la base aérea ...Doña Milla seguía gritando que a su hijo no iba a enterrarlo nadie sin que ella lo viera por última vez. Pero la caja era de plomo y no se puede abrir.

Al otro día enterramos a Moncho Ramírez. Un destacamento de soldados hizo una descarga cuando los restos de Moncho—o lo que hubiera dentro de aquella caja— descendieron al húmedo y hondo agujero de su tumba. Doña Milla asistió a toda la ceremonia de rodillas sobre la tierra.

De todo eso hace dos años. A mí no me había ocurrido contarlo hasta ahora. Es bien probable que alguien se pregunte por qué. Yo diré que esta mañana vino el cartero al ranchón. No tuve que pedirle ayuda a nadie para leer lo que me trajo, porque sé mi poco de inglés. Era el aviso de reclutamiento militar.

TEACHER GUIDE
Memories of Puerto Rico and New York

▶ **OBJECTIVES**

Students will:

1. Describe four customs important to a child growing up in Puerto Rico in the early twentieth century

2. List and evaluate values which shaped Puerto Rican community life

3. Contrast and compare the lifestyle typical of Puerto Rico and of New York City from a migrant's perspective

▶ **QUESTIONS FOR DISCUSSION**

1. When does this story take place? In what kind of an area in Puerto Rico did Mrs. Ríos grow up?

2. What holidays does she remember celebrating? How do they compare to the holidays (religious or non-religious) your family celebrates?

3. Why did Mrs. Ríos leave Puerto Rico for New York?

4. What kind of work did she do in the U.S.? Why?

5. How did Mrs. Ríos and the people with whom she worked try to improve the conditions at their jobs?

6. According to Carmen Clemente, poor people in Puerto Rico were known for what qualities especially?

7. Would Mrs. Clemente be likely to find customs in the U.S. to be similar or different from those she describes? Give examples.

▶ **SUGGESTED ACTIVITIES**

1. On a map of the Caribbean, students locate Puerto Rico and the towns of Ponce and Guayanilla.

2. Students research the masks and costumes associated with Carnival in Puerto Rico. Younger students may enjoy making masks out of paper mache. [You may want to collaborate with an art teacher on this project.] Alternatively, students find pictures of the Three Kings and research the meaning of this Latin American holiday.

3. Students write short essays comparing their own childhood to Minerva Ríos's and Carmen Clemente's experiences of growing up in Puerto Rico. They may include memories of: a baptism (the student's own or someone else's), holidays their family celebrated, school experiences, migration to another country (if their family did this), customs among friends and neighbors.

If there are students in the class who have recently immigrated to the United States, they may identify with these accounts. Encourage them to share their own traditions with the class.

4. Ask students to imagine that they have recently arrived in New York City from Puerto Rico. Each student writes a letter home to friends on the island, telling them what it is like getting used to life in the United States. They should draw on what they have learned about traditional Puerto Rican values and lifestyles.

▶ **RESOURCES**

1. A book suitable for students with an elementary reading knowledge of Spanish is *Aprender A Luchar; Luchar es Aprender*. Puerto Rican women in New York talk about their work, housing, family and community life. Illustrated with photos. Available from the Centro de Estudios Puertorriqueños.

Artist: Rini Templeton

INTRODUCTION
Memories of Puerto Rico and New York

Puerto Ricans who migrated to the United States not only had to leave their homes, families and friends behind. They said farewell to a way of life: one based on a strong sense of community, in which even the poorest people shared the little they had.

Minerva Torres Ríos, 87 years old, came to the United States from Puerto Rico in 1929. For many years she lived in New York City's East Harlem section, one of the oldest Puerto Rican settlements in New York. The people of East Harlem call it simply El Barrio, or "the neighborhood."

Mrs. Ríos was a member of a popular education and literacy program in El Barrio, organized with the help of the Centro de Estudios Puertorriqueños. She reflects in this essay on her childhood in Puerto Rico and subsequent experiences as a laundry worker in New York City.

Carmen Clemente, another member of the El Barrio Popular Education Program, describes the traditions of her people as she remembers them from her childhood in Puerto Rico.

These and other life histories of Puerto Rican women and men were collected by the Centro de Estudios Puertorriqueños, Hunter College, City University of New York.

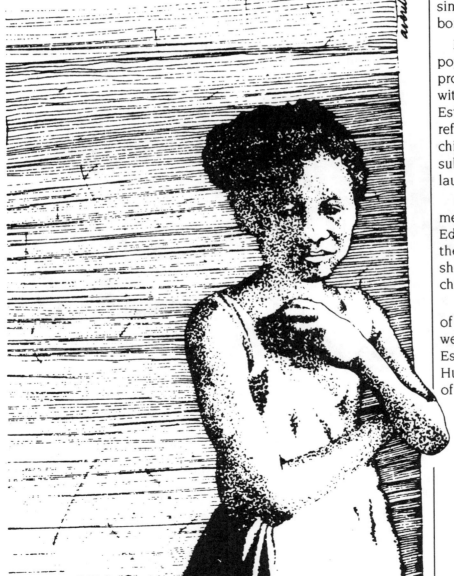

READING
Memories

BY MINERVA TORRES RÍOS

To remember is to live. And how well I remember my childhood in the town of Guayanilla, where I was born June 5, 1905. Guayanilla is in the south of Puerto Rico. It's near Ponce, the second largest city in the country. Other towns nearby are Yauco, famous for its *caracolillo* coffee⁰, and Peñuelas, known for its navel oranges and finger bananas. Peñuelas also has the famous Banana Tree Mountain, one of the five highest mountains in Puerto Rico.

One of my most pleasant memories is of my baptism at age seven. I felt so happy, especially when my godparents pinned a five-*peso* note⁰ to my dress. I knew it was money but I had no idea of its value. At that tender age, just like other Puerto Rican children at the time, I thought two or three cents was more than one dollar and that five *centavos*⁰ was a lot!

Life there was poor, but it was a happy life. You didn't have the violence you have today. We young girls used to go with the boys down to the river and go swimming together with our old clothes on.

The best times of my childhood were the holidays—the patron saints' days⁰, Three Kings' Day and Carnival. For the patron saints' days we got to celebrate for nine days, winding up with a big party in the town square. We'd have games of chance, children's games and most of all, music. Three King's Day, January 6, was a holiday for children, something like the tradition of Santa Claus here in the United States. On that day we would go all around the neighborhood, showing off the presents that the Three Kings had left under our beds. The night before, we would have put a bit of grass under the bed for the kings' camels, who we knew would be tired and would eat the grass hungrily. That's what all Puerto Rican children believed, and I continued to believe in the Three Kings until I was twelve.

Carnival was another time of tremendous enjoyment, especially for children. I remember how we poor people celebrated carnival with water. We'd form groups and throw buckets of water on each other, and we'd put on masks and costumes and dance. We'd parade through the town chanting the famous

Carnival masks. Photos: Jack Délano.

carnival chant: *Vejigante a la bolla, pan y cebolla!*[0]

In 1914 the First World War broke out. I was nine. That's when my suffering began, because my father had to go to war. How I cried to see my father leave me, my brothers and two sisters. Thank goodness, though, my father did not have to serve much time in the military since he was a school teacher and was soon called back to teach.

In 1918, when I was thirteen, I was in school one morning when the whole building began to shake. I had never felt anything like it, and ran screaming for home. I couldn't even stay standing up, I didn't know what to do; everyone was crying, "My God, it's an earthquake!"

The island was left in ruins by that quake. Every town suffered severe damage. There were deaths, and many people were left homeless: my humble house was damaged. They had to use the schools as temporary hospitals. That was the historic earthquake that destroyed much of Puerto Rico.

In school, we used a textbook called *Rudimentos de América*[0], because in those days everything in Puerto Rico used to come from here, from the United States. The governor of the island was American, and the laws were made here.

I know the story of Abraham Lincoln, that they taught me in Puerto Rico; the story of George Washington; Benjamin Franklin with a kite ... They taught some things about Puerto Rico, but there was no textbook on Puerto Rican history. They just taught it orally. They didn't teach us anything about the people of South America. I knew nothing about all that.

I graduated from the eighth grade, which is when you get your first diploma in Puerto Rico. Those who can, go on to study for another four years. But I couldn't continue in school, because there was no high school in my town and I would have had to go to another town and pay. My father and mother had separated by then, and I couldn't afford it.

My mother had to go work in people's houses as a maid, and I worked in a shop embroidering blouses and dresses. The pay was very little. In Puerto Rico at that time poverty was widespread, it was very hard to survive. I decided to come to New York to work in order to help out my mother and siblings. In 1929 I arrived in New York, where the rest of my story takes place.

I left Puerto Rico on a ship called the *Coamo*. There was at that time no other form of transportation between Puerto Rico and the United States. The crossing lasted five days. I spent most of the time up on the deck, in the fresh air to keep from getting seasick. It was quite a pleasant trip and the boat reminded me of a big hotel.

When we reached New York harbor, it was winter and the pier was hidden in fog. We had to wait for two more days outside the port for the weather to clear. Finally the ship sailed into the harbor, and we crossed in front of the Statue of Liberty and you can imagine what an impression that made on me.

A U.S.-run clothing factory in Puerto Rico in the 1950s.

As the ship passed slowly in front of the statue, I wondered to myself why it was there in the water instead of in a park, where everyone could admire it.

The Statue of Liberty was the first marvel I experienced in the City of Skyscrapers. When we disembarked on the Brooklyn pier it was very cold, and I saw another wonder for the first time: snow. I knew what it was, of course, from studying the history of the United States, but I had never seen it personally and to see the ground all covered in white astonished me.

I moved in with my cousin. His wife soon got me a job in a factory where I worked for about six months. In 1930, a friend of mine got me a job working with her in a laundry on East 94th Street. I started out ironing collars and cuffs in the men's shirt department, using huge machines. We worked Monday through Saturday, from 8 a.m. to 7 at night. My salary was $12 per week. The workers in the laundries weren't unionized and so the bosses could do whatever they liked.

On Mondays and Tuesdays we worked until 8 p.m. On holidays we had to work half-days. The summer was when I really suffered, between the work and the heat. When the temperature outside was 90 degrees, it was more than 100 inside the laundry. I sweated miserably between those two ironing machines but what could I do? Nothing but keep on working in order to keep my job. The Depression was gripping the country and there were no jobs; anyone lucky enough to have one wanted to keep it, no matter how small the salary.

Working in a laundry has always been relatively secure employment, although it's one of the hardest jobs. In the days before the struggle to unionize the laundries, the U.S. president passed the National Recovery Act, prohibiting employers from paying less than $14 per week. I'll always remember that great president, Roosevelt.

We began struggling for a union. It took tremendous effort before the bosses would agree to it. They threatened to take away our jobs, but we workers kept on fighting until we won.

We became unionized in 1936 and things began to go better. But it still wasn't easy because the employers didn't want to give us paid vacations. But after a number of years everything improved. We no longer had to work on holidays or Saturdays, and if we did work those days, we received double pay.

I continued working hard from 1930 until 1970, when I retired. By that time, I earned more than $200 a week, with a month of paid vacation.

–Abridged from: Minerva Torres Ríos, "Remembranzas," in *Nuestras Vidas: Recordando, Luchando y Transformando*, produced by the El Barrio Popular Education Program, June 1987. Also includes material from an interview with Minerva Torres Ríos by Rina Benmayor of the Centro de Estudios Puertorriqueños, Hunter College. Translated by C. Sunshine.

Vocabulary

caracolillo coffee: special high-grade coffee bean

five-peso note: five-dollar bill (Although U.S. dollars are the legal currency in Puerto Rico, many people call dollars *pesos*, after the Spanish currency used on the island before 1898.)

five centavos: five cents

patron saints' days: days commemorating Catholic saints. Celebrated like a birthday for children on the day of their namesake; villages and parishes also observe the day of their designated saint.

Vejigante a la bolla, pan y cebolla: Couplet traditionally chanted during Carnival. Its meaning is obscure. *Vejigante*, "giant," refers to the masks which are traditional for Carnival.

Rudimentos de América: "American Basics"

READING
Remembranzas

POR MINERVA TORRES RÍOS

Recordar es vivir: y cómo recuerdo yo mi infancia allá en el pueblo de Guayanilla dónde nací un cinco de junio del 1905. Guayanilla es un pueblo situado al sur de Puerto Rico. Sus pueblos vecinos son Ponce, la

su famosa montaña, una de las cinco mas grandes que hay en Puerto Rico y que se llama Mata de Plátano.

Tengo un grato recuerdo y fué cuando me bautizaron a los siete años. Me sentí muy felíz y

tierna edad, creí que dos o tres centavos valían más, pues en Puerto Rico en aquel entonces cinco centavos yo los veía eran mucho y creo que iqual le pasaba los otros niños también.

La vida allá fue pobre, pero

Woodcarvers made statues of the Three Kings.

Ciudad Señorial de Puerto Rico y la segunda más grande. Después le sigue Yauco, famoso por su café caracolillo y luego Peñuelas famosa por sus chinas injertas, guineitos manzanos, y

contenta, cuando mis padrinos prendieron un billete de cinco pesos en el trajecito que llevaba puesto. Yo sabía que eso era dinero pero no sabía el valor del mismo. Yo ignorante a mi

fue una vida contenta y alegre, por la cuestión de que no había la violencia que hay hoy en día. Nosotros con los muchachos nos íbamos p'allá p'al río, nos bañábamos juntos con vestidos viejos puestos.

Los días más felices y alegres de mi infancia eran las fiestas patronales, el Día de los Santos Reyes y el Carnaval. En las fiestas patronales tenía la dicha de gozar de nueve días felices y contenta pues teníamos fiesta en la plaza, picas, juegos juveniles, y sobre todo música para deleitarnos. El Día de los Reyes, ese era un día de alegría de los niños como lo es el día aquí de "Santa Claus." Los niños en Puerto Rico el Día de los Reyes, que es el seis de enero, se nos veía corriendo por todo el vecindario enseñando lo que los tres Reyes nos dejaron debajo de la cama después, que el día antes nosotros le habíamos puesto un macito de yerba para que sus camellos que venían cansados y con hambre comieran. Eso era creencia de nosotros los niños allá en Puerto Rico y que yo creí hasta que tuve doce años de que era verdad que existían los tres Santos Reyes.

El carnaval era otro tiempo de felicidad para todo el mundo, especialmente para los niños. Yo me acuerdo que los pobres jugábamos y celebrábamos el carnaval con agua. Nos juntábamos grupos y nos echábamos baldes de agua unos a otros y también haciamos bailes y nos poníamos caretas y disfraces y caminando por todas partes diciendo algo muy famoso del carnaval: "vejigante a la bolla, pan y cebolla."

En el mil novecientos catorce (1914) estalló la guerra mundial. Yo tenía 9 años. Y entonces empezaron mis sufrimientos pues mi padre tuvo que partir para la guerra. Cómo lloré y sufrí al ver a mi padre separarse de su familia, ya eramos dos hermanos y tres hermanas. Mi padre gracias a Dios no estuvo mucho tiempo en el servicio militar pues como él había sido maestro de escuela y el pueblo se quedó escaso de maestros él fué licenciado con otros más.

Tenía yo trece años, en mil novecientos diez y ocho (1918). Y a las once de la mañana empezó todo en la escuela a temblar y yo, como nunca había experimentado una cosa así, corrí gritando para mi casa. No podía estar en píe en la tierra. Yo no sabía qué hacer y todo el pueblo gritaba: "Dios mío es un fuerte temblor de tierra."

La isla de Puerto Rico quedó en ruinas. Todos los pueblos sufrieron mucho. Hubo muertes, gente quedaron en la calle sin casas. Mi pobre y humilde hogar quedó averiado, y por un tiempo las escuelas tuvieron que servir de hospitales. Bueno, ese ha sido el temblor de tierra que ha hecho en Puerto Rico que destruyó a nuestra Isla y a su gente.

En la escuela nosotros teníamos un libro allá que se llamaba Rudimentos de América, porque en aquel tiempo todo era de Estados Unidos. Allá entonces el gobernador era americano, las leyes eran hechas aquí.

Yo sé la historia de Lincoln, que me la enseñaron en Puerto Rico; la de Washington; Benjamin Franklin estaba con una chiringa ... Sí, había clase de las cosas de Puerto Rico, pero no había un libro de historia de Puerto Rico. Lo enseñaban oral.

Allá en Puerto Rico no nos enseñaron nada de los mayas, ni de esta gente de Sur América. Nada de eso yo sabía.

Me gradué de octavo grado, pues hasta ese grado era que daban en Puerto Rico el primer diploma, después el que podía seguir estudiando los otros cuatro años seguía. Para mí fué muy imposible seguir en la escuela pues mi padre se había separado de mi madre y en mi pueblo no había escuela superior y tenía que ir a otro pueblo y pagar, y eso yo no pude hacer.

Mi madre tuvo que irse a trabajar en trabajos domésticos y yo fuí a trabajar a un taller bordando y calando blusas y trajes. El sueldo era muy poco. En Puerto Rico para aquel tiempo no había mucho ambiente para uno vivir. Era mucha la pobreza. Yo decidí venir a Nueva York a trabajar y ayudar a mi madre y hermanos. Llegué a Nueva York un día en el mil novecientos veintinueve (1929). El resto de mi historia se basa en Nueva York.

Salí de Puerto Rico en un barco llamado "El Coamo," pues

para aquél entonces no había otro medio de transportación entre Puerto Rico y Estados Unidos. Cinco días duró la travesía. Yo me pasé la mayor parte del tiempo afuera en popa, cogiendo el fresco y para no marearme mucho. Fue un viaje muy placentero pues uno se encontraba como si estuviera en un gran hotel.

Cuando llegamos al puerto de Nueva York, nos encontramos con un poco de dificultad debido a que por ser un tiempo invernal el muelle estaba muy nublado y el barco no podía anclar. Dos días estuvimos fuera del puerto esperando que el tiempo estuviese claro. Por fín llegó la hora de seguir marcha hacia el puerto y el barco se movía por el frente de la Estatua de la Libertad y qué impresión tan grande me causó. Según el barco pasaba despacio frente a la estatua, yo la miraba y me decía para mí misma, y no podía imaginarme por qué esa estatua no la tenían en un parque en vez de tenerla allí en el mar, pues en un parque todo el mundo podía verla.

La Estatua de la Libertad fue la primera maravilla que experimenté en la Ciudad de los Rascacielos. Desembarcamos por el muelle de Brooklyn y hacía mucho frío, y por primera vez vi otra maravilla que fue la nieve. De ésa sí me admiré pues yo sabía de ella por lo que estudié en la historia de América, pero como nunca la había visto personalmente, al ver todo el suelo cubierto de blanco en verdad que me impresionó.

Fuí a vivir con mi primo. Al poco tiempo la esposa de él me llevó a trabajar a una factoría y estuve allí como seis meses. En el mil novecientos treinta, una amiga me llevó a trabajar a un "laundry" al este de la calle noventa y cuatro.

Nos costó mucho trabajo para que los patronos aceptaran unionarse.

Empecé a trabajar planchando cuellos y puños en el departamento de camisas de hombre, en unas máquinas grandísimas, de lunes a sábado, de ocho de la mañana a siete de la noche. Mi sueldo era doce pesos semanales. Los "laundries" no tenían unión y los patronos podían hacer lo que ellos quisieran.

Lunes y martes teníamos que trabajar hasta las ocho. Los días feriados teníamos que trabajar medio día. En el verano era que yo más sufría, el trabajo por un lado y el calor por otro. Cuando la temperatura estaba afuera a noventa grados, dentro del "laundry" estaba a más de cien. Yo sudando en medio de aquellas dos máquinas pero ¿qué podía yo hacer? Nada, sino seguir mi tarea para asegurar mi trabajo. La

depresión azotaba el país y no se encontraba trabajo, y el que lo tenía aunque fuera ganando poco tenía que asegurarlo.

El trabajo de los "laundry" ha sido siempre lo más seguro, aunque lo más duro. Antes de que los trabajadores empezaran a luchar por unionar a los que trabajamos en los "laundries", el presidente para aquel entonces pasó una ley llamada N.R.A. (National Recovery Act), la cual prohibía a los patronos que pagaran menos de catorce pesos a sus empleados. Siempre recuerdo a ese gran presidente Roosevelt.

Llegó la lucha de pelear por la unión. Nos costó mucho trabajo para que los patronos aceptaran unionarse. Nos amenazaron con dejarnos sin trabajo, pero nosotros los empleados seguimos la lucha hasta que vencimos.

En el mil novecientos treinta y seis quedamos unionados y todo empezó a arreglarse, pero no todo fue muy fácil pues después los patronos no nos querían dar vacaciones y pagarlas. Después de varios años todo fue mejor. No trabajábamos días feriados ni sábados y si lo hacíamos nos tenían que pagar doble.

Seguí trabajando fuerte desde el mil novecientos treinta hasta el mil novecientos setenta cuando me retiré del trabajo. Ya para este tiempo yo ganaba alrededor de más de doscientos pesos semanal y un mes de vacaciones pagas.

READING
The Traditions of My People

BY CARMEN CLEMENTE

The poor people of my country were known for their generosity. When you cooked the mid-day meal, for instance, you would call over your neighbor and present her with a plate of the cooked food. It didn't matter that the neighbor would have cooked a meal too. It was the custom, and every good-hearted Puerto Rican followed it.

When December rolled around every family would have a piece of pork meat for Christmas, because those households that could afford to slaughter a pig would share the meat with their neighbors. Families who had harvested crops from their garden, like *gandules*°, bananas, *yautía*°, and sweet potatoes, also shared with their neighbors. So every Puerto Rican family could put good things on the table at Christmas time: *arroz con gandules*°, *chicharrones*°, yautía, and cakes. And all this without spending the kind of money one has to spend today!

I remember from my childhood how kind we were to each other, much more so than today. Nowadays, all that's left of the old customs is that a household that keeps a pig will often collect leftover food from their neighbors in order to be able to feed it. Then, when Christmas comes and the pig is slaughtered, they repay the families that contributed with a portion of the meat. Times have changed because the cost of living has gone up so high.

And yet even today, Puerto Ricans as well as outsiders who visit the Island know they won't die of hunger. Because you still have good-hearted people who inherited humility and generosity from their parents and grandparents. May these ways continue among our Puerto Rican and Latin American people!

Vocabulary

gandules: pigeon peas (small round beans)

arroz con gandules: rice and beans

yautía: starchy root vegetable

chicharrones: pork cracklings

Artist: Rini Templeton

READING
La persona humilde de Puerto Rico

POR CARMEN CLEMENTE

La persona humilde de mi patria era persona de buen corazón. Cuando ellos hacían almuerzo lo que se hacía llamar a la vecina para darle un plato de comida. No le importaba que la vecina tenía también que comer, pero eso era una costumbre que todo puertorriqueño de buen corazón y humilde tenía de costumbre.

Llegaba el mes de diciembre que era el de navidad y todas la casas tenían un pedazo de carne de cerdo. Porque si se mataba un cerdo, se repartía con la vecina. El que tenía su siembra, como gandules, guineo, yautia y batata, también repartía con los vecinos. Y el arroz con gandules, los chicharrones, la yautía y los pasteles no faltaban en la mesa de los puertorriqueños en ese día de navidad. Y no había que gastar tanto dinero como lo que hay que gastar hoy en día.

Recuerdo mis años de infancia, ver tanta bondad que había en los corazones de las personas humildes que hoy en día no lo hay. Ahora lo único que se acostumbra es el que tiene cerdo va para la casa y recoge la comida de cerdo y cuando llega la fecha tan sagrada que es la navidad, mata un cerdo y se lo reparte a las personas durante el año. Pero el tiempo tenía que cambiar con tanto que ha subido el costo de la vida.

Pero todos los puertorriqueños como los extranjeros que llegan a Puerto Rico saben que allí no se muere de hambre porque siempre hay personas de buen corazón que heredan la humildad y el corazón de sus padres y abuelos.

Que viva Puerto Rico y todos los países de habla hispana. Gracias.

-Reprinted from: Carmen Clemente, "La Persona Humilde de Puerto Rico," in *Nuestras Vidas: Recordando, Luchando y Transformando*, produced by the Programa de Educación Popular de El Barrio, June 1987. Translated by C. Sunshine

Artist: Rini Templeton

TEACHER GUIDE
La Bomba and La Plena, Music of Puerto Rico

▶ **OBJECTIVES**

Students will:

1. Identify four cultural influences which contributed to the development of the *bomba* and *plena*

2. Explain the role *plena* played in Puerto Rican community life

3. Give examples of how music can help sustain a people's culture and values across generations

▶ **QUESTIONS FOR DISCUSSION**

1. Why would music similar to the *bomba* exist in Jamaica and Haiti?

2. What are some of the different cultural influences in the *bomba*? In the *plena*?

3. What function did drumming have for Africans during their enslavement? Why?

4. Who was Bumbún Oppenheimer? How did he help develop the *plena*?

5. What topics typically were used for *plena* songs?

6. Why do you think the rich people didn't like the *plena*?

▶ **SUGGESTED ACTIVITIES**

1. It is important to the enjoyment of this unit that students have the opportunity to hear *bomba* and *plena* music. You are encouraged to obtain tapes or records for classroom listening, either through the mail-order sources listed below (see Resources) or at a record store.

Before assigning the reading, play for the class examples of several of the following: West African music, Puerto Rican *plena*, salsa, Jamaican reggae, Dominican *merengue*, Cuban *son*, Trinidadian steelband. Ask them to listen for and list similarities and differences.

2. Show the film, *Plena Is Work, Plena Is Song*. (See Resources.)

3. Divide the class into teams of two students each. Each team chooses an event that happened in the school or community. They are to compose a *plena* about it and sing it for the class. They should remember to make their songs humorous!

▶ **RESOURCES**

1. *Bomba* and *plena* music on record and compact disk can be ordered by mail from: Original Music, RD #1, Box 190, Lasher Road, Tivoli, NY 12583. Tele-

phone (914) 756-2767. They carry other types of Caribbean music as well. A free catalogue provides a partial listing of items in stock; customers may also ask for a complete listing for the type of music they are seeking.

The Ethnic Folk Arts Center, 131 Varick St., Room 907, New York, NY 10013, offers a tape cassette of *bomba* and *plena* music entitled "Puerto Rico, Puerto Rico - Mi Tierra Natal" (cassette #65001.) Telephone (212) 691-9510.

2. *Plena Is Work, Plena Is Song/Plena, Canto Y Trabajo* is a 36-minute color documentary focusing on the relationship between the Puerto Rican working-class experience and musical expression. Produced and directed by Pedro Rivera and Susan Zeig, in Spanish with English subtitles. Available from Cinema Guild.

3. Three films available from the Centro de Estudios Puertorriqueños:

• *Machito: A Latin Jazz Legacy* documents the influence of Latin music on jazz through the story of the musician Machito. Other jazz legends, including Tito Puente, Dizzy Gillespie, and Ray Barretto also appear. 58 minutes, color, 16mm film or VHS.

• *Percussions, Impressions and Reality* examines the role traditional music plays in maintaining cultural unity of Puerto Ricans in the U.S. and in Puerto Rico. 30 minutes, color, 16 mm film or VHS.

• *Salsa: Latin Pop Music in the Cities* features performances, interviews and recording sessions with leading salsa musicians. Videotape.

INTRODUCTION
La Bomba and La Plena, Music of Puerto Rico

Of all the African traditions brought to the Caribbean, music, along with religion, most completely survived the plantation experience. Often in defiance of planter prohibitions, the slaves sang, danced and played drums, passing on these important African cultural customs to their children

As a result, African music provided a foundation for Caribbean music as it developed into its modern forms. Steelband in Trinidad, reggae in Jamaica, *merengue* in the Dominican Republic and Puerto Rican *plena* all reflect the strong drum rhythms of Africa.

The *bomba* is a traditional drum-dance which originated among Puerto Rican slaves in the colonial period. Drums were made from empty grease barrels, with a goatskin stretched over the top. As Puerto Rican musician Jorge Arce explains, the *bomba* is related to drum-dances in other Caribbean cultures, reflecting common African roots.

Around the beginning of the twentieth century, the *bomba* combined with other musical influences to produce the *plena*. The *plena* is also based on drum rhythms. The musician holds the drum, or *pandereta*, in one hand and strikes it with the other. Another instrument used is the *güiro*, which is made from a dried gourd with ridges carved on the side. The musician rubs

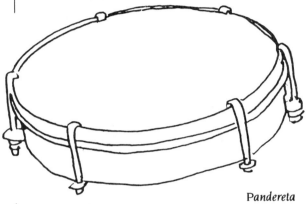

Pandereta

a stick against the ridges to produce a scraping sound. The guitar and harmonica are also used.

As in the *bomba*, a singer sings verses and a chorus responds, a typically African form known as "call and response." The words to *plena* songs typically offer witty social commentary on current events. In "Bumbún and the Beginnings of La Plena," Juan Flores describes the *plena*'s roots in the life experiences of the Puerto Rican working class.

Güiro

Maracas

READING

La Bomba Is an Original Puerto Rican Creation

BY JORGE ARCE

The *bomba* came to Puerto Rico with the slaves from Africa. It came with the Ashanti people, who arrived here in the 15th, 16th and 17th centuries.

We have to remember that when the Africans were brought to the Americas, the different groups were divided up and sent to different places. Not all the Ashanti° ended up in Puerto Rico; many went to other islands. So you have a dance very similar to the *bomba* in Jamaica, for example. I once saw a group of Jamaican children using barrels as drums, beating them with two sticks and doing dance steps much like our *bomberos*° do.

We had a delightful experience when we went to visit the Haitian refugees here at Fort Allen°. We took them a drum as a present, and they began to play. When I saw what they were doing, I said, "Hey, what's this!" It wasn't precisely the same as our *bomba*, but there was an obvious connection.

The *bomba* brings together elements from various cultures. You have Spanish influences in the dancing style and the way the female dancer swirls her skirt. There is Arawak° influence in the use of the *maracas*°, which keep the rhythm along with the drums. African influence accounts for most of the rest: the instruments, dance steps and singing. The words to the songs are in Spanish, of course, but with an African rhythm and intonation. All this combines to make the *bomba* an original Puerto Rican creation.

Historians believe that the slaves used the *bomba* to send messages, and even to plan entire revolts. We don't know exactly how they did it. We do know, though, that the slaves who organized the revolts were most often the ones brought recently from Africa. They spoke different African languages, and they didn't speak much Spanish yet; so to organize the other slaves, what could be more logical than to use movement? In the *bomba*, the dancer chooses a step and the drummer follows. So the dance could be a symbol, could send a message.

–Adapted from an interview with Jorge Arce by Kris Eppler, San Juan, Puerto Rico, 1983.

Vocabulary

Ashanti: a West African people living mainly in Ghana

bomberos: bomba musicians

Fort Allen: U.S. federal detention center in Puerto Rico, where the U.S. government has detained Haitian refugees

Arawak: indigenous people who lived on Puerto Rico before the arrival of the Europeans

maraca: rattle made from a gourd which is dried with the seeds inside

READING
Bumbún and the Beginnings of la Plena

BY JUAN FLORES

The Puerto Rican *plena* arose at the beginning of this century in the sugar-growing areas along the southern coast of the Island. Within a generation, it came to be recognized as the most authentic and representative music of the Puerto Rican people.

When *plena* was first emerging from its folk roots, the pioneer and king of *plena* was Joselino "Bumbún" Oppenheimer (1884-1929). The name Oppenheimer, an unlikely one for a Black Puerto Rican worker, was adopted from German immigrant plantation owners, and attests to his slave ancestry. The nickname "Bumbún" echoes the thudding beat of his *pandereta*, the tambourine-like hand drum used in *plena*.

Bumbún was a plowman. For years he drove oxen and tilled the fields of the huge sugar plantations outside his home city of Ponce°. In the mornings he would leave La Joya del Castillo, the Ponce neighborhood where he lived, and be off along the paths and byways leading to the plantation. He hitched up the plow and prepared the oxen for the day's work. Then he was joined by the *cuarteros*, the young laborers who helped the plowman by walking ahead to keep the oxen moving and by clearing the furrows of stones and cane stubble. Bumbún's *cuarteros*

Woodcut by José Rodríguez

were always in earshot, though, for they also served as his chorus. He sang to the beat of ox and mule hooves and the rhythmic thrust of the plow:

No canto porque me oigan
I don't sing because anyone listens

Ni porque mi dicha es buena
Nor because they tell me it's good

Yo canto por divertirme
I sing to entertain myself

Y darle alivio a mis penas.
And to ease my burdens.

Bumbún composed many *plenas* while tilling the fields of the Hacienda Estrella plantation. Patiently he would teach the choruses to his plowboys. They would repeat them in energetic response as Bumbún went on to sing the solo verses of his new song.

After work, Bumbún would make his way home to La Joya del Castillo. There, at night, he would introduce his latest compositions to the many *pleneros*° and fans who gathered in the small wooden houses and storefronts of the neighborhood. Bumbún led the first *plena* band and became the first professional *plenero* when he decided to set down his plow and dedicate full time and energy to music.

All the early *pleneros*, including

Bumbún, were originally *bomberos*. The *plena's* most basic musical features come from the *bomba*. These blended with other types of Puerto Rican music, especially the *seis* and the *danza*, to form the *plena*.

Influences from other Caribbean cultures also played a role. After the abolition of slavery in the British colonies, many former slaves drifted to other islands in the region, looking for work. Families from the British Caribbean islands of Jamaica, Barbados, St. Kitts and Nevis, among others, came to Puerto Rico. Many settled in the sugar-growing areas around Ponce.

They brought with them musical styles which were different and exciting to the native *ponceños*[0]. These new sounds fused with musical traditions native to Puerto Rico. The so-called "English" sound caught on in Ponce and helped spark the emergence of *plena*.

In the early decades of the century, many former slaves, peasants and craftsmen were becoming wage laborers on large corporate plantations. Many *plenas* tell of strikes and other important events in workers' lives. Because of its working-class character and loud drum beat, the upper class initially scorned the *plena* as "primitive" and "vulgar noise."

Many workers migrated, and the *plena* took root in New York's Puerto Rican community by the late 1920s. As some of the best-known *pleneros* left, drawn by the lure of recording possibilities, New York City became the center for further development of the *plena*. The New York newspaper *El Nuevo Mundo* noted the music's popularity: "At night in our Latin neighborhood, oozing out of the cracks in the windows and blasting from the music stores, there is the sound of the Puerto Rican *plena*, which has taken over everywhere, from the poorest and filthiest tenements of East Harlem to the most comfortable middle-class apartments on the West Side."

As it achieved commercial success, the *plena* came to be accepted by all social classes in Puerto Rico as an authentic "national" music. But its humble beginnings should not be forgotten. When Bumbún Oppenheimer composed his songs while driving an ox-drawn plow across the canefields, rehearsing his verses with his chorus of plowboys, he established the roots of *plena* in the process of human labor. It was work and the life experiences of working people that gave birth to *plena*, and shape its development to the present day.

—Adapted from: Juan Flores, "Bumbún and the Beginnings of la Plena," in *Centro*, Vol. II, No. 3, published by the Centro de Estudios Puertorriqueños, Hunter College.

Vocabulary

Ponce: second-largest city in Puerto Rico

pleneros: *plena* musicians

ponceños: inhabitants of Ponce

READING
Plena Is Work, Plena Is Song

Pleneros in El Barrio, New York City. Photo by Carlos de Jesús from the film Plena Is Work, Plena Is Song.

The Puerto Rican Plena Is All About Life ...

"The Puerto Rican *plena* is all about life, see? Things that happen, incidents of all sorts: love, jail, prison, deception, rip-offs ... Whatever's going on gets into the *plena*.

They cut up Elena
They cut up Elena
They cut up Elena
And they took her
To the hospital!
Don't be afraid, dear one

I've come to tell you
They cut up Elena, mama
I'll never forget her!"

— Marcial Reyes, *plenero*

"If there was a crime, if a girl ran off with her boyfriend, if a man beat his wife—this happened a lot—all this would get recorded in *plenas*."

— Antonia Vásquez, garment worker

"The *plena* tells stories newspapers don't print. Instead, you make up verses, set them to music and sing. That's *plena*."

— Shorty Castro, T.V. personality

"When a guy really liked a woman and wanted her to know, instead of just talking, he'd sing her a *plena*.

You say you don't love me
So much the better, say I
Less dogs! Less fleas!
So why offer your love?"

— Papo Rivera, *plenero*

The Tun-Tun-Tun Disturbed Their Ears

"The rich people didn't want our music to become popular. But today, it travels all over the world.

The rich lived up above the poor neighborhoods. They knew they could get action, so they'd call the police and complain: 'Those black people down there are partying and dancing and we can't sleep! Do something about it!' Those rich people were used to violin music, so the 'tun, tun, tun' disturbed their ears! They had money so the police would come, beating people up and smashing their drums. Folks ended up with their heads bashed in, but they had to keep quiet or they'd be arrested for disturbing the peace."

— Rafael Cepeda, *plenero*

They're On Strike at Puerta de Tierra

"The San Juan docks were always full of action. The dockworkers had the best chance to unionize, so that's where Santiago Iglesias° began organizing and helped them fight for better wages. They earned damn little—ten or fifteen *pesos*. The bosses treated workers like slaves. So they fought back. And the *pleneros* at Puerta de Tierra wrote a *plena* that went like this:

They're on strike
at Puerta de Tierra!
All the dockworkers have
stood up in protest!
Out come the scabs
all over the island.
The workers, all of them
have stood up in protest!
They're on strike
at Puerta de Tierra!
All the dockworkers have
stood up in protest.
Santiago Iglesias says
'Fight until we win!'
'Cause they're on strike
at Puerta de Tierra.
All the workers proclaim
they're out in protest!"

— Rafael Cepeda, *plenero*

How Plena Is Formed

"A people who speak, cry and suffer hardship, also find joy. We tie all these feelings into one, and that is how *plena* is formed."

— Rafael Cepeda, *plenero*

The Plenero Has To Be a Voice of Protest

"As a kid I was too young to understand the *plena*. But, I started going with my father to his gigs. We also played *plenas* at home every day. And he taught me the beat during his breaks, giving me the background to each song. I learned all I could and once I got the hang of it, I realized that *plena* would be my life too.

We've been working here for years. We lived here and helped build those buildings—the Banco Popular, Chase, Citibank, Banco Central, the Federal Court and the Free School of Music. We worked on those buildings for years. And now we're being kicked out, and it hurts.

The *plenero* has to be a voice of protest. He has to defend his people.

A lament I am singing
A sad lament in my voice.
I lament for my neighborhood
Now destroyed and gone."

— Papo Rivera, *plenero*

–Spanish and English dialogue from: *Plena Is Work, Plena Is Song/Plena, Canto Y Trabajo*, color documentary film produced and directed by Pedro Rivera and Susan Zeig. English subtitles by Rina Benmayor.

Vocabulary

Santiago Iglesias: noted Spanish trade union leader who organized in Puerto Rico in the early 20th century

READING
Plena, Canto Y Trabajo

La plena es lo que ha pasado en la vida

"O sea, la plena puertorriqueña es ... lo que ha pasado en la vida, ¿me entiende? Hechos que pasaron, muchas formas, en el amor, en cárceles, presidio, desengaño, traición, robo ... Entonces, eso crea a la plena. Por ejemplo:

Cortaron a Elena
Cortaron a Elena
Cortaron a Elena
Y se la llevaron p'al hospital.
No te asustes, cosa buena
Porque te vengo yo a hablar.
Cortaron a Elena, mamá
No la puedo olvidar."

— Marcial Reyes, plenero

"Si había un crimen, si había una muchacha que se fue con el novio, si el marido peleaba con la mujer y le daba un pela— pues eso sucedía mucho— cualquier cosa que pasaba, pues le sacaban una plena."

— Antonia Vásquez, trabajadora

"Porque la plena son historias, son historias que no aparecen en los periódicos, que se ponen letras, melodías y se canta. Esa es la plena."

— Shorty Castro

"Sabes, eso era cuando a la persona le gustaba la tipa y quería decirle algo, o sea, quería hablar con ella, pero quería decirle algo cantando.

Tu dices que no me quieres
Yo digo mucho mejor
Menos perros, menos pulgas
¿Porque me brinde tu amor?"

— Papo Rivera, plenero

Ese tún, tún, tún, le molestaron...

"La gente que tenía el dinero estaban en contra de que nuestra música, que hoy en día se pasea por todos los sitios, estuviera.

Pues ellos vivían en ciertos sitios donde más abajo vivían pobres. Y ellos por la tranquilidad que podían, ellos decían a la policía: "Vayan, que allá están bailando esta gente negra y no dejan dormir aquí a la gente!" Esa clase de personas que no están acostumbradas que a oir música de violin y de cosas, al sentir ese tún, tún, tún, tún, tún, tún, le molestaron. Y entonces ellos, como era gente pudiente, mandar a la policía ... por si la policía llegaba sin preguntar, pues caían a palos a la gente y muchos se iban al hospital con la cabeza rajada y tenían que quedarse callados porque si decían algo en seguida, pues, lo denunciaban por traición a la paz."

— Rafael Cepeda, plenero

Hay huelga en Puerta de Tierra

"Pues resulta que en los muelles de Puerta de Tierra siempre hubo movimiento. Allí fue donde Santiago Iglesias Pantín principió a hacer el obrerismo en Puerto Rico. El trabajador de los muelles fue la persona más indicada para poder luchar para levantar su dinero, que ganar más dinero. Entonces él luchó para que ese trabajador se ganara más dinero para poder vivir. Porque ganaba muy poco, muy poco dinero, porque ellos al coger el trabajador y esclavizarlo pues le daban diez, quince o lo que fuera. Tenía que seguir luchando por eso. Entonces, hasta sacaron una plena en Puerto de Tierra, que decía:

¡Hay huelga
En Puerta de Tierra!
Por causa de los trabajadores
Están en protesta.
Y salen los rompehuelgas
De la isla entera.
Los trabajadores
Toditos están en protesta.
¡Hay huelga
En Puerta de Tierra!
Los trabajadores
Toditos están en protesta.
Si dice Santiago Iglesias
Hay que luchar.
Pero hay huelga
En Puerta de Tierra.
Y dicen los trabajadores
¡Toditos están en protesta!"

— Rafael Cepeda, plenero

Así se forma la plena

"El pueblo que habla y que sufre y que llora cuando pasa algo, pero que siempre tiene alegría ... Y el sufrimiento que ha pasado forma la alegría y entonces que se forma la plena."

— Rafael Cepeda, plenero

El plenero tiene que ser protestante

"Cuando yo estaba muy chiquito no entendía nada de la plena porque estaba un niño todavía. Entonces, empecé a salir con mi papá para arriba y para abajo, para ir a diferentes sitios a tocar plena. Pero en casa se tocaba plena todos los días. Mi papá siempre me explicó bien la plena. Me enseñaba a mí el golpe, y me decía el por qué de esta plena.

Yo trataba de entender hasta que dí, y entonces yo supe que esa nota a mí me gustaba.

Nosotros hemos trabajado aquí muchos años. Nosotros hemos ayudado a construir esos edificios a pesar de que hemos vivido aquí—el Banco Popular, el Chase Manhattan, el Citibank, Banco Central, la Corte Federal, el Instituto Libre de Música. Trabajamos todos en esos edificios y por muchos años. Nos duele mucho tener que movernos pa' otro lado, ¿ve?

El plenero tiene que ser protestante por su país, porque tiene que defender lo suyo ¿entiende?

Lamento yo voy cantando
Lamento se oye mi voz
Lamento porque mi barrio
Ya desapareció."

— Papo Rivera, plenero

Dancing the bomba.

TEACHER GUIDE
The Customs and Traditions of the Tabaqueros

▶ **OBJECTIVES**

Students will:

1. Describe the practice of "factory reading" introduced into the United States by Caribbean cigar-makers

2. Evaluate purposes for the readings

3. Predict possible results this practice may have had on the lives of the cigar-makers

▶ **QUESTIONS FOR DISCUSSION**

1. How did Bernardo Vega and his fellow cigar-makers continue their education while they worked? Why do you think they tried so hard to continue learning?

2. If you worked in a factory, would you want someone to read to you? If so, what reading materials would you select? Why?

3. What do you know about the authors mentioned and their writing? Why do you think the cigar-makers chose these authors? Why might the subjects be of interest to the workers?

4. The reading and discussion that Vega described no longer go on in most factories and workplaces. Why do you think this is so? Is this good or bad? Why?

5. Compare Bernardo Vega's experience of working in the U.S. to that of Minerva Ríos (Unit 2). Which would you prefer?

▶ **SUGGESTED ACTIVITIES**

1. Bring in a cigar. Unwrap it to show the tobacco leaves inside. A member of the class can research and report on how cigars are made, including any changes in the manufacturing process since Vega's day.

2. Each student interviews a relative to find out how, when and why members of their family came to the United States. What did they do when they arrived? Did they work, pursue an education or both? What kinds of challenges did they face, and how did they resolve them? Students can write short essays or stories based on their findings. [Note to the instructor: Family histories may be a delicate subject for some students and their families. The instructor needs to use her/his own judgement in adapting this exercise for a particular class.]

▶ **RESOURCES**

1. *El Legado: A Puerto Rican Legacy* is a 30-minute film tracing the growth of the Puerto Rican community in New York during the early 20th century. Includes interviews with early migrants. 16 mm or VHS. Available from the Centro de Estudios Puertorriqueños.

2. Three books available from the Centro de Estudios Puertorriqueños:

• Jesús Colón, *A Puerto Rican in New York and Other Sketches* (International Publishers, 1982). Short essays and anecdotes by a Puerto Rican cigar-maker who came to New York in 1918.

• César Andreu Iglesias, ed., *Memoirs of Bernardo Vega* (Monthly Review Press, 1984). Pictures the political and social life of the early Puerto Rican community in New York. Suitable for senior high and above.

• Juan Flores, ed., *Divided Arrival: Narratives of the Puerto Rican Migration 1920 - 1950* (Centro de Estudios Puertorriqueños, no date). Short excerpts from Colón and Vega (see above), and two other Puerto Rican emigrant authors. Bilingual text in English and Spanish.

An American-owned cigar factory in Puerto Rico in the early twentieth century.

INTRODUCTION
The Customs and Traditions of the Tabaqueros

When Bernardo Vega came to the United States from Puerto Rico in 1916, it was his first time leaving the island of his birth. He traveled by himself on the steamship *Coamo*, ready to make a new life in New York. "I hadn't the slightest idea what fate awaited me," he recalls.

He remembers vividly his arrival as the boat docked in New York harbor:

First to disembark were the passengers traveling first class—businessmen, well-to-do-families, students. In second class, where I was, there were the emigrants, most of us tabaqueros, or cigar workers. We all boarded the ferry that crossed from Staten Island to lower Manhattan. We sighed as we set foot on solid ground. There, gaping before us, were the jaws of the iron dragon: the immense New York metropolis.

All of us new arrivals were well dressed. I mean, we had on our Sunday best. I myself was wearing a navy blue woolen suit (or flus as they would say back home), a borsalino hat made of Italian straw, black shoes with pointy toes, a white vest, and a red tie. I would have been sporting a shiny wristwatch too, if a traveling companion hadn't warned me that in New York it was considered effeminate to wear things like that. So as soon as the city was in sight,

"There, gaping before us, were the jaws of the iron dragon: the immense New York metropolis." Artist: Manuel Otero

and the boat was entering the harbor, I tossed my watch into the sea ... And to think that it wasn't long before those wrist-watches came into fashion and ended up being the rage!

Bernardo Vega joined a growing community of Puerto Rican immigrants in New York City. He had worked as a cigar-maker in Puerto Rico from an early age, and in New York he again found work in a cigar factory. In this excerpt from *The Memoirs of Bernardo Vega*, he describes how he and the other cigar-makers continued their education while they worked.

READING

The Customs and Traditions of the Tabaqueros and What It Was Like to Work in a Cigar Factory in New York City

BY BERNARDO VEGA

One day my friend "El Salvaje" took me down to Fuentes & Co., a cigar factory located on Pearl Street, near Fulton Street, in lower Manhattan. I started work immediately, but within a week they had marked down the price of my make of cigar°, and I quit.

A few days later I found work at another cigar factory, "El Morito" ("The Little Moor"), on 86th Street off Third Avenue, a few steps from where I was living. At that wonderful place I struck up friendships with a lot of Cubans, Spaniards, and some fellow countrymen, all of whom awakened in me an eagerness to study.

With workers of this caliber, "El Morito" seemed like a university. At the time the official "reader" was Fernando García. He would read to us for one hour in the morning and one in the afternoon. He dedicated the morning session to current news and events of the day, which he received from the latest wireless information bulletins.

The afternoon sessions were devoted to more substantial readings of a political and literary nature. A Committee on Reading suggested the books to be read, and their recommendations were voted on by all the workers in the shop. The readings alternated between works of philosophical, political, or scientific interest, and novels, chosen from the writings of Zola, Dumas, Victor Hugo, Flaubert, Jules Verne, Pierre Loti, Vargas Vila, Pérez Galdos, Palacio Valdes, Dostoyevsky, Gogol, Gorky, or Tolstoy. All these authors were well known to the cigarworkers at the time.

It used to be that a factory reader would choose the texts himself, and they were mostly light reading, like the novels of Pérez Escrich, Luis Val, and the like. But as they developed politically, the workers had more and more to say in the selection. Their preference for works of social theory won out. From then on the readings were most often from books

Bernardo Vega

by Gustave LeBon, Ludwig Buchner, Darwin, Marx, Engels, Bakunin ... And let me tell you, I never knew a single *tabaquero* who fell asleep.

The institution of factory readings made the *tabaqueros*

...there was always someone who insisted on going to the *mataburros* or "donkey-slayers"...

---

into the most enlightened sector of the working class. The practice began in the factories of Vitas & Co., in Bejucal, Cuba, around 1864. Of course there were readings before then, but they weren't daily. Emigrants to Key West and Tampa° introduced the practice into the United States around 1869.

In Puerto Rico the practice spread with the development of cigar production, and it was Cubans and Puerto Ricans who brought it to New York. It is safe to say that there were no factories with Hispanic cigarworkers without a reader. Things were different in English-speaking shops where, as far as I know, no such readings took place.

During the readings at "El Morito" and other factories, silence reigned supreme—it was almost like being in church. Whenever we got excited about a certain passage we showed our appreciation by tapping our tobacco cutters on the work tables. Our applause re-sounded from one end of the shop to the other. Especially when it came to polemical matters no one wanted to miss a word. Whenever someone on the other side of the room had trouble hearing, he would let it be known and the reader would raise his voice and repeat the whole passage in question.

At the end of each session there would be a discussion of what had been read. Conver-sation went from one table to another without our interrupting our work. Though nobody was formally leading the discussion, everyone took turns speaking. When some controversy re-mained unresolved and each side would stick to a point of view, one of the more educated workers would act as arbiter. And should dates or questions of fact provoke discussion, there was always someone who insisted on going to the *mataburros* or "donkey-slayers"—that's what we called reference books.

But life among the *tabaqueros* was not all serious and sober. There was a lot of fun too, especially on the part of the Cuban comrades. Many were the times that, after a stormy discussion, someone would take his turn by telling a hilarious joke. Right away tempers would cool down and the whole shop would burst out laughing.

None of the factories was without its happy-go-lucky fellow who would spend the whole time cracking jokes. In "El Morito" our man of good cheer was a Cuban named Angelito, who was known for how little work he did. He would get to the shop in the morning, take his place at the worktable, roll a cigar, light it, and then go change his clothes. When he returned to the table he would take the cigar from his mouth and tell his first joke. The co-workers nearest him would laugh, and after every cigar he'd tell another joke. He would announce when he had made enough cigars to cover that day's rent. Then he'd set out to roll enough to take care of his expenses. Once this goal was reached, he wouldn't make one more cigar, but would leave his workplace, wash up, get dressed, and head for the Broadway theaters.

–Abridged from: César Andreu Iglesias, ed., *Memoirs of Bernardo Vega* (Monthly Review Press, 1984). Translated by Juan Flores.

Vocabulary

my make of cigar: Cigar prices varied according to the "make"—the quality of the tobacco and the cigar-maker's reputation.

Key West and Tampa (Florida): early centers of cigar production in the U.S.

TEACHER GUIDE
Arturo Alfonso Schomburg

▶ **OBJECTIVES**

Students will:

1. Summarize the important points in the life of Arturo Schomburg

2. Explain why Schomburg, a Puerto Rican, collected books on Black history

3. Analyze contributions made by Schomburg to American life and culture

▶ **QUESTIONS FOR DISCUSSION**

1. What do Puerto Ricans look like? Schomburg was Black but there are light-skinned Puerto Ricans too. Why?

2. Describe two incidents in Schomburg's life in which he was confronted with racism. How did he respond? Do you think this was effective, or not? Why?

3. Why did Schomburg decide to collect books on Black history? Why did he think it was important to teach Black students about their heritage?

4. What are some of the achievements for which Schomburg is remembered?

▶ **SUGGESTED ACTIVITIES**

1. Students find out more about the life and work of Arturo Alfonso Schomburg. New York-area students can visit the Schomburg Center; others can write to the Center for information. Address: Schomburg Center for Research in Black Culture, The New York Public Library, 515 Malcolm X Boulevard, New York, NY 10037. (212) 862-4000.

▶ **RESOURCES**

1. Elinor DesVerney Sinnette, *Arthur Alfonso Schomburg: Black Bibliophile and Collector* (New York Public Library and Wayne State University Press, 1989). Authoritative, readable biography with an extensive bibliography.

2. Flor Pineiro de Rivera, ed., *Arthur Alfonso Schomburg: A Puerto Rican Quest for His Black Heritage. His Writing Annotated with Appendices.* (San Juan: Centro de Estudios Avancados de Puerto Rico y el Caribe, 1989). Available from Casa de la Herencia Cultural Puertorriqueña.

INTRODUCTION
Arturo Alfonso Schomburg

Many Puerto Ricans who migrated to the United States were dark-skinned, and they suffered racial discrimination. Some responded by stressing their Hispanic identity. But Arturo Alfonso Schomburg was proud of his dual heritage as Latino and Black.

Schomburg was born in Puerto Rico in 1874. His father was a German merchant living in San Juan and his mother a Black woman from the Virgin Islands. Schomburg's experiences as a child in Puerto Rico helped inspire his determination to fight racism, as Epifanio Castillo and Valerie Sandoval recount in "Our Forgotten Scholar."

Young Schomburg came to the United States in 1891, at age 17. For several years he lived in the Puerto Rican community in New York City. Around 1900, he moved to the African-American neighborhood of Harlem, and became deeply involved in the Black literary and artistic movement known as the Harlem Renaissance. Victoria Ortiz explores this period of Schomburg's life in "Schomburg and the Harlem Renaissance."

Schomburg dedicated his life to preserving and disseminating the historical record of peoples of African descent. He urged schools and universities to establish courses in Black history. He collected books and documents from far and wide, dealing with all aspects of Black history and culture. His personal collection of some 5,000 books and 3,000 manuscripts, plus countless pamphlets and photos, became the core of the famous Schomburg Center for Research in Black Culture, located in New York City.

READING

Arturo Alfonso Schomburg: Our Forgotten Scholar

BY EPIFANIO CASTILLO JR. AND
VALERIE SANDOVAL MWALILINO

With a few exceptions, the Puerto Ricans who came to New York City before 1898 are a forgotten group. That is a pity. It should be a well-known fact that many Puerto Ricans migrated to the city before their Island was annexed by the U.S. as a "booty of war," and that several of them made important contributions to their adopted nation. One such early settler was Arturo Alfonso Schomburg, a historian and scholar who became so eminent in other fields that his Latino[0] heritage has been all but ignored.

His name still blazes, of course, among U.S. Blacks. Schomburg was an opponent of discrimination throughout his long, eventful life. He avoided militancy, preferring to marshall historical facts to his cause. As a result of his work, Blacks found old precedents in their fight against prejudice and new pride in their heritage.

Schomburg also ranks as the greatest collector of books on Black culture. The Schomburg Center for Research at the New York Public Library, which he founded, contains an astonishing 75,000 volumes on the subject. His strictly Latino activities were less extensive and less well known. But the fact is that Arturo Schomburg was always vitally interested in Latinos, their freedom and well-being.

The seed which was to flourish throughout Schomburg's life was planted in his mind while he was still in Puerto Rico. It seems that one of his teachers stated that the Negro had never accomplished anything in the past and probably never would in the future. Schomburg was so outraged by this racist attack that he set out to disprove it by finding significant works by Black Puerto Ricans. What he was looking for, he said, were the contributions of the "Colored Races" to the development of Western civilization. That became his lifelong search.

The young scholar accumulated quite a collection of books and pamphlets about the African experience in Puerto Rico. Whenever he heard a slur, such as the one his teacher made, Schomburg could easily rebut it by bringing up any number of examples, including those of José Campeche, the artist whose portraits caused a major sensation in Italian art circles, and Rafael Cordero, the impoverished cigarmaker who was also one of Puerto Rico's pioneer educators. Schomburg not only intended to combat racial discrimination wherever he found it—even though the problem, while present, has never been severe in Puerto Rico—but also to build pride in his people. The writer Floyd J. Calvin put it this way: "When his white associates began to tell of what history white Puerto Ricans had made, [Schomburg] could talk equally freely of the history Black Puerto Ricans had made."

There is no record of the Latino's feelings on arriving in New York in 1891. Surely he must have been aghast at the racial prejudice he encountered. For this was a time when racism was perhaps at its most stark in the U.S. Blacks—and Black Latinos—were not supposed to have an equal chance to succeed, especially in intellectual realms. Arturo Alfonso Schomburg, of course, already had proof that they could succeed.

His was not an easy path. For his first five years in New York, young Arturo studied law at the offices of Pryor, Mellias and Harris. Unhappy with the practice of law, he joined the Bankers Trust Co. Beginning in the page and messenger department, he worked his way up until, when he retired from the bank, he had become the head of the mailing division in the

Arturo Alfonso Schomburg

Latin American department. That was the highest position that any Black could achieve in those days.

On the other hand, Schomburg's rather undemanding job allowed him to travel and search for materials to add to his ever-growing collection. One ironic story concerns a trip Schomburg took to the deep South. Denied hotel accommodations because of his color, he promptly sued—and won because he spoke fluent Spanish. According to one of his sons, the authorities decided that "Negroes in the South were Negroes, but if a Negro was a Puerto Rican, he wasn't a Negro." Schomburg often identified himself as "a Puerto Rican of African descent," though never to escape narrow definitions of Negritude[0]. He was simply proud of his past.

A quiet, serene man, he seldom spoke unless he felt that he had something worth saying. As a result, he was greatly esteemed by his peers. The honors flooded in. This is not the place to report them all, but a short list would include Schomburg's presidency of the American Negro Academy at Howard University, a stint at Fisk University and his time as curator of the collection which bears his name; he also founded the Negro Society for Historical Research.

Arturo Alfonso Schomburg died in 1938, leaving a large family. Of his nine children, the last three were given Latino names: Dolores, Fernando and Carlos. Clearly, Schomburg never forgot that he was a Latino, and there is no question but that his early Puerto Rican experiences molded his future life and actions. Because of his more than apparent African blood, he felt a double duty to combat prejudice in whatever form it took. His example as a quiet fighter against prejudice— and his exemplary humanismo[0]— still can inspire all Latinos today.

–Abridged from: Epifanio Castillo Jr. and Valerie Sandoval Mwalilino, "Arturo Alfonso Schomburg: Our Forgotten Scholar," Nuestro, May 1978.

Vocabulary

Latino: Latin American; Spanish-speaking; Hispanic

Negritude: cultural/literary movement stressing the dignity and worth of the African heritage

humanismo: love of humanity

READING
Schomburg and the Harlem Renaissance

BY VICTORIA ORTIZ

I am here with a sincere desire to awaken the sensibilities, to kindle the dormant fibers in the soul, and to fire ... racial patriotism by the study of ... Negro books ... It is the season for us to devote our time to kindling the torches that will inspire us to racial integrity.

Arthur Schomburg spoke these words in July 1913 to a group of Afro-American teachers attending summer courses at the Cheney Institute, in Pennsylvania. In this presentation he outlined the intellectual foundations of the period known as the Harlem or Black Renaissance. Urging his listeners to consider the importance of teaching Black students about their heritage, about their African and Afro-American roots, Schomburg went on:

There have been written many histories of our people in slavery, peace and war, each one serving a purpose. These books have been useful to disseminate the fragmentary knowledge to localities, where the spark of learning has awakened the soul to thirst for more and better food ... These [books] have been our landmarks, our rock of ages, let us place around them the inspiring love so that the scholars of today ... will be spurred to do things by which we will be remembered, and in the coming days will be heralded for

racial identity, racial preservation and racial unity ... We need in the coming dawn [someone] who will give us the background for our future ... give us, with trenchant pen, the story of our forefathers and let our soul and body ... brighten the chasm that separates us.

The fervor in Arthur Schomburg's words grew from his deep sense of outrage at the wrongs perpetrated against Black people, not least of which was, in his opinion, the denial of their heritage and history. Like many of his contemporaries, Schomburg saw history as a weapon with which to fight injustice against the race, a tool to build a future of dignity.

Despite a full-time work schedule at the Bankers Trust Company and the responsibilities of a family man, Arthur Schomburg participated in all aspects of Harlem's social, cultural and political life during the development and apogee of the Harlem Renaissance. This period, from approximately 1920 to 1930, was one of lively artistic and cultural regeneration in the Black community. It confirmed once and for all the fact that Afro-Americans have historically enriched the culture of this country with expressions at once different from and linked to the mainstream culture.

Harlem became the center for the extraordinary creation of works of literature, music, graphic art, sculpture, theater, and historiography. Once its reputation as a Black cultural mecca was established, Harlem attracted scores of Afro-American, Caribbean, and African artists, writers, students, intellectuals and others, all inspired by the community's creative genius and eager to participate in its flowering. The poet Langston Hughes, himself one of the shining lights of the Harlem Renaissance, described the life-giving social and cultural home that was Harlem:

Harlem, like a Picasso painting in his cubistic period. Harlem— Southern Harlem—the Carolinas, Georgia, Florida—looking for the Promised Land—dressed in rhythmic words, painted in bright pictures, dancing to jazz—ending up in the subway at morning rush time—headed downtown.

West Indian Harlem—warm rambunctious sassy remembering Marcus Garvey°. Haitian Harlem, Cuban Harlem, little pockets of tropical dreams in alien tongues. Magnet Harlem, pulling in an Arthur Schomburg from Puerto Rico, pulling in Arna Bontemps all the way from Carolina, a Nora Holt from way out West, an E. Simms Campbell from St. Louis, likewise a Josephine Baker, a Charles S. Johnson from Virginia, an A. Philip Randolph from Florida, a Roy Wilkins from Minnesota, an Alta Douglas from Kansas. Melting pot Harlem— Harlem of honey and chocolate and caramel and rum and vinegar and lemon and lime and gall.

The men and women involved in Harlem's cultural movement sought to express and examine all of the concerns that had developed over the past fifty years of growing tension between the Black and white societies. They were delineating new attitudes toward blackness, developing the concept of race pride, returning to look at and learn from Black folk roots. They were rediscovering the deep ties they had with Africa ... Arthur Schomburg's contribution was to provide materials, interpretation and insights on Black achievements past, present and future.

In addition to providing the Afro-American community with valuable historical information through his articles, book reviews and bibliographies, Arthur Schomburg made other contributions to the Harlem Renaissance. According to those who knew him personally, he was a gregarious and generous man, always available to help guide younger writers and students in their quest for Black history ... He loaned his books, allowed people into his home to use his materials, and spent long hours discussing favorite topics. Furthermore, although his own financial situation was never very good, he never denied assistance to those in need, especially if they were young Afro-American students, writers, artists or musicians.

Schomburg also wrote often to newspaper and journal editors, politicians, and scholars in the United States and abroad. He wrote to publishers criticizing them for signs of prejudice in their dictionaries or encyclopedias; he wrote to editors protesting against articles that distorted the Black experience; and he wrote to intellectuals or political leaders questioning their interpretation of some aspect of Black history.

–Abridged from: Victoria Ortiz, "The Legacy of Arthur Alfonso Schomburg: A Celebration of the Past, A Vision for the Future." Published by the Schomburg Center for Research in Black Culture, The New York Public Library.

Vocabulary

Marcus Garvey: Jamaican Pan-African leader who based his movement in Harlem in the 1920s

TEACHER GUIDE

Our Mothers' Struggle Has Shown Us the Way

▶ **OBJECTIVES**

Students will:

1. Describe typical work experiences of Puerto Rican women who migrated to the U.S. in the 1940s and 1950s

2. Explain why some U.S. companies relocate their factories abroad and analyze consequences for workers in the United States and other countries

3. Predict the results of these work experiences on the lives of Puerto Rican migrants

▶ **QUESTIONS FOR DISCUSSION**

1. How much was Lucila Padrón paid in Puerto Rico to hand-sew dresses that sold for $100 in department stores in New York? Why the discrepancy?

2. Why did many Puerto Rican women take jobs in garment factories in the U.S.? How did they deal with problems on the job?

3. Why did many Puerto Rican women lose their factory jobs? Do any other workers in the United States face similar problems today? Why might companies choose to move their factories to other countries?

4. How do the young women interviewed feel about what their mothers and grandmothers experienced? How has it affected their lives?

▶ **SUGGESTED ACTIVITIES**

1. Show the film "Global Assembly Line." (See Resources.) After viewing the film, discuss question #3 above with the class.

2. Students examine the labels on their clothing to determine where it was made, then locate these countries on a world map. As a research project, the class may try to find out how much garment workers earn in these countries.

3. Invite a representative of a garment workers' union to talk with the class. Students should prepare in advance questions based on the reading and class discussion. If possible, ask a clothing company representative to respond to the same questions, either in person or through an exchange of letters. Two unions representing garment workers in the U.S. are:

- International Ladies Garment Workers Union, 1710 Broadway, New York, NY 10019.

- Amalgamated Clothing and Textile Workers Union, 15 Union Square West, New York, NY 10003.

▶ **RESOURCES**

1. The Centro de Estudios Puertorriqueños contains the largest collection in the country of publications, films and videos, newspapers and journals, photographs and other materials on the Puerto Rican experience in the United States. It is located in Hunter College, at 68th Street and Lexington Avenue in New York City.

2. "Nosotras Trabajamos en la Costura: Puerto Rican Women in the Garment Industry" is a bilingual radio documentary produced by Rina Benmayor, Ana Juarbe, Blanca Vázquez Erazo (1985). It is available as a 30 minute bilingual cassette from the Centro de Estudios Puertorriqueños. Also available is "Nosotras Trabajamos en la Costura," a 15 minute slide show in English and Spanish versions. Rental from Centro de Estudios Puertorriqueños.

3. *Global Assembly Line*, a 56 minute color documentary film, focuses on women factory workers in Mexico and the Philippines and the impact on U.S. workers when factories move overseas. Available from New Day Films.

4. "Extended Roots: From Hawaii to New York: Puerto Rican Migration to the U.S." Collection of essays about Puerto Rican migration to different parts of the United States. Available from the Centro de Estudios Puertorriqueños.

INTRODUCTION

Our Mothers' Struggle Has Shown Us the Way

The late 1940s began the period of mass migration from Puerto Rico to the United States under "Operation Bootstrap." Many women who came found work as sewing machine operators in garment factories in New York City, where pay and working conditions were often poor. The women played an important role in the effort to unionize the factories and win better conditions for workers.

Manufacturers, however, soon found it more profitable to move their factories overseas, where they could take advantage of even cheaper, non-union labor. After 20 or 30 years of work, many Puerto Rican women lost their jobs when factories "ran away."

A group of women, some of them the daughters and granddaughters of garment workers, decided to find out more about this part of their community's history. Working with the Oral History Task Force of the Centro de Estudios Puertorriqueños, they interviewed former garment workers. From these interviews they produced a radio documentary, "Nosotras Trabajamos en la Costura." They explain:

> This program is about our mothers and grandmothers, the thousands of Puerto Rican women who spent their working lives as seamstresses in the garment factories of New York City. These are some of their stories, that we at the Center for Puerto Rican Studies at Hunter College have been collecting. This is an effort to document and explain our history, to ourselves, to our own communities, and to those who may want to share our lives.

"nosotras trabajamos en la costura..."

Puerto Rican Women In The Garment Industry

READING
Puerto Rican Women in the Garment Industry

• *My mother is an embroiderer. She does such beautiful, intricate work. She's been doing that for 20 years now, ever since she came to this country. She raised me and my three sisters all by herself. And she doesn't speak English, to this day.*

• *My grandmother learned to sew in Puerto Rico when she was a little girl, sewing and embroidering fancy lingerie for an American company. Then she came to New York in the twenties, and she was a pionera°, and she spent all her life in a garment factory.*

• *We came to New York in 1948. My father drove a cab, and my mother worked in a garment factory for 30 years. Just last Christmas she was laid off permanently. And now she has to find a job, at the minimum wage. That's a hard life, and it's happening to a lot of our parents.*

When Puerto Rico became a colony of the United States in 1898, American clothing manufacturers didn't waste much time. By 1915, they had set up a whole needlework° industry on the island. There they could escape from the unions and make bigger profits by using the labor of women and children.

Lucila Padrón is now in her seventies. She clearly remembers what her childhood was like.

It was awful. I was born in Ponce, Puerto Rico. That's where I was raised and went to school. I started doing needlework when I was a little girl, in order to help my parents, because we were poor. After the housework and school, instead of playing, we had to sew. It was a sacrifice.

Lucila and her sisters started working at home. Local contractors would distribute bundles of fabric already cut and ready to be sewn to women all across the island. The women would return the finished products beautifully sewn and embroidered, all by hand. Then the work was shipped to New York and sold in exclusive department stores like Wanamaker's or B. Altman's.

Our work was really something to see. It was all done by hand—no machines. Tracing, embroidering, assembling, all of it by hand. And do you know what they paid us? For all that intricate work? Later on, when I came to New York, I saw the clothes we made selling in Wanamaker's on 14th Street. Here, those robes or dresses sold for $100 or more. There, they used to pay us for one of those dresses, with all that embroidery—three dollars. So, to earn ten or twelve dollars a week, we had to work day and night.

Lucila was a teenager when she came to New York in 1927.

She wanted to continue her education, but instead she had to support herself and then her own family.

When I came to New York, I had a hard time at first, because I couldn't find a sewing job. I used to walk back and forth, across Manhattan, from shop to shop, from one end of the island to the other, until I finally found a job as a seamstress ... I worked in garment factories for 30 years, working so I could get where I am now and give my children an education. And I'm very proud of that.

Like Lucila, many of our grandparents migrated to New York during these early years looking for work. Some had been driven off the land by American sugar monopolies. Cigar-makers, carpenters and other skilled workers came too.

By 1930 there were over 50,000 Puerto Ricans in the United States. Men, women and entire families came. The journey took five days by boat, and most people settled in East Harlem°, or along the Brooklyn waterfront.

Luisa López came as a child in 1923 on the steamship *Coamo*.

My mother and father came to get us at the boat, and when I came into the apartment I found my brother at a machine, sewing. What was he doing?

Artist: Manuel Otero

Coffee bags. Everybody used to help my mother; that machine was going on all day long.   I was sewing, my sister was sewing, my brother was sewing, everybody to help out.

Sewing meant economic survival for many Puerto Rican families. During the Depression, Luisa and her sister went to work in garment factories. Puerto Rican women were the newcomers, competing for jobs with Italian and Jewish women.

I was working in a shop called Elfran's Dress Company, in El Barrio°, on 104th Street. The Italian girls, they wanted to sit down, and the rest of the girls refused to work, because they didn't want to work with Puerto Ricans. When I saw that, I went to the union, and I spoke to the manager, and I told him what had happened. This manager over here was Italian, he was an old-time socialist, the most wonderful person you ever came to know. His name was Joe Piscatello. He called everybody to the union. And I explained to him, "You know, I'm more an American citizen than some of these people are, that don't even know how to speak English." He gave them hell! He gave them hell! So we all went back to work.

By 1937, the International Ladies Garment Workers Union° had more than 2,000 Puerto Rican members. Ironically, just a few years later in the early forties, Luisa lost her union job, in a way that forecast what would happen to thousands of garment workers in the seventies and eighties.

His name was Mr. Cohen. And he opened up five shops in Puerto Rico, that's how come I lost my job. We belonged to the union over here, he had to pay us higher wages. While in Puerto Rico at that time, he could pay fifteen and twenty cents an hour.

After World War Two, U.S. manufacturers were offered big tax breaks to set up factories in Puerto Rico. This was part of Operation Bootstrap, the plan to industrialize the island. But these new factories, many of them garment and light industry, never provided enough jobs. So although industry was busy relocating to the island, by the end of the sixties close to a million Puerto Ricans had migrated to New York.

This was our mothers' generation. Our parents settled with family or friends, in furnished rooms or tenement apartments, in East Harlem, the Lower East Side, or the South

Bronx...

In the 1950s, the garment industry in New York was booming. Puerto Rican women were hired by the thousands as sewing machine operators, one of the lowest paying jobs in the trade. Although many of our mothers were already experienced needleworkers, by this time the garment industry no longer needed such fine skills. Clothing production was changing. Seamstresses used to make whole garments, but now, women were sewing only sections in assembly-line fashion.

Section work is sewing zippers, or collars. When I first came to this country, I was sewing the whole garment. But later, I found section work. Because working sections, you can make a lot more money. And I was fast.

Section work allowed New York garment manufacturers to increase production. And this new, cheap labor pool meant they could also increase their profits. Thousands of Puerto Rican and black women became low-paid, unskilled section workers—easily exploited, and easily replaced. Because wages were so low, women like María Rodríguez often brought home extra work, even though home work was illegal.

The boss let me take bundles home, and I used to do it at night. I'd work two hours, three hours to make a little more money. And some times weekends I used to take it, and Victor used to help me. I'd teach my husband how to do it, so he used to help me to do the bundles also. So then, I'd make about $35, sometimes $38.

Many women, like Dolores Juarbe, found themselves working in sweatshops—small, non-union operations in firetrap buildings which violated minimum wage laws, paid no overtime, sick leave, or vacation.

There was not any union there. In that shop you had to sew, as fast as you could. And everyone smoked. The shop was in a basement. Once in a while the fire department would pay a little visit. The boss told us to stop smoking, that the fire department was on the way. The alerter heard that they were coming, you know, she used to pay them off. So then, they could knock real loud on the door: bam bam bam! And all the cigarettes would disappear.

Not only were our mothers subjected to these poor working conditions, some even had to fight off the boss.

I did not like the boss. The boss could not keep his hands off the girls. He was always walking in and touching them and squeezing them. So one day, he came to me, and like he tried to feel me up, and I told him, "Listen," I said. "I don't like you. I don't like this job, I don't like the way you treat the girls. So you can keep it!" I got ready to leave. "Oh, don't go, don't go." "Oh no," I said. "You are a pig!"

Many Puerto Rican women looked for union shops where they expected to get protection, benefits and higher wages. During the fifties, labor unions were stepping up their organizing, and many of our mothers and grandmothers led that effort. Some became union chairladies and organizers, and sometimes the chairlady had the power to stop the shop.

Eva Monge remembers how she shut down her housecoat factory to support a dressmakers' strike.

The dresses were going on strike. The boss right away stopped the housecoats and gave us dresses. The first day, I said, "All right, but ..." I noticed that the strike kept on. So, on the second day I said, "Mrs. Corey, every girl on this shop is going to finish the bundle that they're doing. They're not going to make no more dresses." You know, that boss went to the dressing room and she cried! But it was from anger. She knew that she was wrong—she was breaking the strike.

By the 1960s Puerto Rican women made up over 25 percent of New York sewing machine operators. The rank and file of the garment unions was now overwhelmingly Puerto Rican and Black. But despite their numbers and their histories of activism, few Black or Puerto Rican women find themselves in positions of power. For decades, the top union leaders have been conservative white men.

Gloria Maldonado is a business agent for ILGWU Local 22-89-1. But she is an exception.

I'm the only woman here. The only woman officer, and the only Hispanic business agent. The manager is Puerto Rican, but I'm the only woman. So I'm Puerto Rican, I'm a woman and I'm Black. I've got three affirmative action points (laughs).

... During the fifties and sixties, our mothers' work gave our families some economic stability. But then, things began to change. Over the last 30 years, well over 200,000 garment jobs have left New York City alone. And so operators have dwindled to a bare minimum in factories like Juanita Erazo's, where older, higher-paid workers are the first to go.

My friend María, she's been working for him for 29 years, just like me. She was the first one he laid off. That's how he discriminates! He gets rid of the one who earns more money, and those are the older and more experienced operators. The boss just spent three weeks in Taiwan, and he came back loaded down. The factory is four stories high, and practically all the floors are filled with that imported work. What he wants to do is turn the factory into a shipping department, and get rid of the operators altogether. Because the work comes already finished, and ready to sell.

Today, garments are cut in New York, sewn in Taiwan, Korea or Mexico, finished in Puerto Rico, and sent back to New York for distribution. An operator in Haiti is paid 21 cents an hour, for what in New

York costs over $3.00.

As they learned with the Puerto Rican model in the thirties and again in the fifties, clothing manufacturers find it even more profitable today to set up shops in Asia, Latin America and the Caribbean. Gloria Maldonado describes just how massive this relocation is.

Some of these countries, they do a lot of needlework. And

capital people, they saw the advantage of making good money, at the expense of other people's misery. And at the expense of our people working here. Big firms started going out, and little by little they started expanding, expanding, until before we knew it ... It used to be maybe two, three garments out of ten that were imported. Now it's five or six out of ten. The shops are not the ones that are running away, it's the manufacturers. For instance, our Joe Namath, you know, big shot Joe Namath, has a line of men's clothes. Where is he getting it done? China. The thing is, that even though they're made there for less money, it's not sold here for less money like years back.

... While manufacturers take their capital abroad, our mothers face widespread layoffs, which often deprives them of their pensions. After years at the machines, many of our mothers suffer back and leg pains, or they are crippled by arthritis.

At the same time, thousands of poor women are migrating to the United States, hoping to escape poverty and often, political repression in their countries. They become cheap labor in factories and sweatshops. Many are undocumented[0] and live in fear of deportation. Juanita Erazo was horrified by a recent immigration raid on her factory in Brooklyn.

In the factory there are Dominicans, Ecuadorians, Colombians and Haitians. The last time Immigration[0] raided, they took everyone away. They took Puerto Ricans away too. They handcuffed them, they filled two buses up with people. Then, after they left, the boss went looking around, and there were people hiding in boxes!

As a union official, Gloria Maldonado has seen how all of this has affected our mothers' generation.

People are just not making it. The small shops are closing up, and that's where it affects our people, our generation, of Puerto Rican women who are not old enough to retire, but have put in 20, 30 years. They stay with this one little shop because it was like a family. All of a sudden, the man has to close because there is no work ...

These are the women who raised us. They were not only our mothers and grandmothers, but our cousins, aunts, neighbors, friends. They went to the factories early in the morning and sat in front of those machines day after day. They confronted the difficulties of migration, poverty, low pay, discrimination, and unstable jobs. In spite of that, they raised us and kept our families together. They fought for our education, organized in the communities and on the job, and they gave us a legacy of struggle.

My mother's work set the tone in the family, set the tone for hard work and struggle. She never missed a day of work, which used to amaze us. She was there at 8:00 in the morning, she came home at 5, 5:30, by the time she came in from Brooklyn. And what she always said to us was, "You have to study. You have to study so that you could be a teacher, you could be a nurse." And we knew what it meant to us, so that we did study. We got somewhere because she worked so hard. Now I know that that's not true for a lot of Puerto Ricans, I know that for the majority of Puerto Ricans, working hard hasn't led to success.

All these stories are a chapter in our history, which for the most part has yet to be told. Our mothers and grandmothers shared their lives with us, so that we could understand more clearly where we are today.

–Abridged from radio documentary: "*Nosotras Trabajamos en la Costura*/Puerto Rican Women in the Garment Industry," produced by Rina Benmayor, Ana Juarbe, Kimberly Safford and Blanca Vázquez Erazo (Centro de Estudios Puertorriqueños, Hunter College, 1985). Program funded in part by National Endowment for the Humanities. Bilingual cassette available

Vocabulary

pionera: pioneer

needlework: sewing and embroidering by hand

East Harlem: one of the oldest Puerto Rican settlements in New York City

El Barrio: East Harlem

International Ladies Garment Workers Union: trade union representing workers in the clothing manufacturing industry

undocumented: without legal documents proving one's right to be in the United States

Immigration: the Immigration and Naturalization Service of the U.S. government

TEACHER GUIDE
Operation Bootstrap's Legacy

▶ **OBJECTIVES**

Students will:

1. List reasons why "Operation Bootstrap" was implemented

2. Contrast and compare the positive and negative consequences of industrialization in Puerto Rico

3. Consider possible alternatives to Operation Bootstrap for building Puerto Rico's economy

▶ **QUESTIONS FOR DISCUSSION**

1. What was "Operation Bootstrap"? Who designed the plan? Why? (Refer to "A Brief History of Puerto Rico" for more information.)

2. What were some of the positive economic results of Operation Bootstrap? How did these affect the lifestyle of Puerto Ricans?

3. What were two main problems associated with Operation Bootstrap?

4. Why aren't federal environmental regulations strictly enforced in Puerto Rico?

5. Doña Licha states that "They benefit from the smoke; I benefit from the stamps." What does she mean by this? Who is "they"? Do all Americans benefit from the smoke? Who does benefit from it? Is Doña Licha content with the arrangement? How do you know?

6. How have people like Purita Gil Pérez responded to the pollution problem? Do you think their response was reasonable? Was it effective? What other alternatives may they have had for dealing with the problem?

7. Are there benefits to having factories such as the Du Pont plant in the area? How would a representative from Du Pont be likely to answer this question? What about a member of the Mayor's committee in Manatí? What do you think?

8. Consider major environmental issues in the U.S., such as toxic waste disposal, nuclear power, smog, oil spills. Have any of these affected your community? How did people react?

▶ **SUGGESTED ACTIVITIES**

1. Invite a speaker from an environmental organization to discuss how pollution affects the environment. Alternatively, invite a science teacher from your school to address the same topic. The class should choose one incident, such as the Bhopal tragedy, the Three Mile Island nuclear accident, or the Exxon oil spill in Alaska, to examine in depth. Students

should submit questions to the speaker in advance.

2. The class debates the following question: "Pollution is a necessary price to pay for economic growth. Yes or No?" Break into small groups for the debate, representing:

a) U.S. companies operating in Puerto Rico

b) Puerto Rican community groups

c) Puerto Rican government officials

d) U.S. unions

e) Puerto Rican unions

Each team should prepare for the debate by researching the issue and formulating logical and persuasive arguments. Preparation might include contacting the public relations offices of companies with factories in Puerto Rico (Du Pont may be contacted at 1-800-441-7515). For the perspective of community and environmental groups, contact Puerto Rico Industrial Mission, P.O. Box 3728, San Juan, PR 00936. Telephone 809-765-4303.

▶ **RESOURCES**

1. Alfredo López, *Doña Licha's Island: Modern Colonialism in Puerto Rico* (South End Press, 1987). Portrait of contemporary Puerto Rican society, presenting a critical view of the island's U.S. ties.

2. *Manos a la Obra: The Story of Operation Bootstrap* is a 59-minute color film on the transformation of Puerto Rican society under Operation Bootstrap. Available from Cinema Guild. A study guide to accompany the film is available from the Centro de Estudios Puertorriqueños.

3. *Puerto Rico: Paradise Invaded* is a 30-minute color film on the history and contemporary realities of Puerto Rico, from a pro-independence perspective. In Spanish with English subtitles. Available from Cinema Guild.

INTRODUCTION

Operation Bootstrap's Legacy

Freeways crisscross the capital, their familiar green-and- lifestyle, enjoyed by many San Juan residents, is one side of capita, than any country in the world.

At the Plaza Las Américas shopping center in San Juan. Photo: C. Sunshine

white signs provided by the U.S. Federal Highway Administration. A giant shopping mall, Plaza Las Américas, beckons the consumer with an array of goods. Afterwards, shoppers can stop in at Dunkin' Donuts, Pizza Hut or McDonald's for a snack.

This Americanized consumer Operation Bootstrap's legacy.

Puerto Rico has the second highest per capita income in Latin America, although its income level is far below that of the poorest U.S. state, Mississippi. Literacy and life expectancy approach U.S. levels. The island imports more goods from the United States, per

But Operation Bootstrap, the ambitious plan to industrialize Puerto Rico, has another side as well. Along the island's north coast, chemical and pharmaceutical plants owned by U.S. companies spew toxic wastes into the ocean. In the south, oil refineries and petrochemical plants darken the air with soot. Twelve percent of all illegal toxic waste dumps in the U.S. are in Puerto Rico, an island less than half the size of Massachusetts.

Federal environmental laws apply to Puerto Rico, but they are rarely enforced. Indeed, freedom to pollute is a major attraction for foreign companies in Puerto Rico. When criticisms are raised, U.S. and Puerto Rican officials point out that the Puerto Rican economy depends on foreign investment.

But industrialization has also had economic costs. The island's fishing industry has been nearly destroyed. In "Doña Licha's Island," Puerto Rican writer Alfredo López pictures the impact of pollution on a fishing community.

Another major impact has been on public health. Purita Gil Pérez lives near the town of Manatí on the island's north coast. The Du Pont company manufactures chemicals in a large factory complex outside Manatí, piping wastes into a treatment plant. Residents of the area have experienced respiratory ailments which they attribute to waste leaking from the pipes.

In 1985 Du Pont planned a new plant which would produce herbicide using phenyl sulphonyl isocyanate, a potentially hazardous chemical. Alarmed, residents of communities around the Du Pont complex tried to stop the company from building the plant. Purita Gil Pérez talks about their experience.

Du Pont ultimately built the plant. The company hired Burson Marsteller, a public relations firm based in Washington, DC, to overcome community opposition to the project. Divisions within the Manatí environmental committee also weakened its effort. But similar campaigns are underway in towns all around the island, and the issue of environmental pollution remains a serious one for Puerto Rico's future.

READING
Doña Licha's Island

BY ALFREDO LÓPEZ

Doña[0] Licha suspected that the devil brought the waves of fish to her island in 1974.

Each day, Licha would stuff a shopping bag with canvas cloth and walk the four winding miles down her hill and up the road to the beach where the palm trees arch stiffly out of the sand and the small stores sell fresh fish and vegetables to the people in cars from the nearby highway.

There she would watch as dawn's light uncovered the water line and the bodies of fish appeared, oily and decomposed from the heat of the water. As the tide receded, more fish appeared. They came up by the thousands that year: black, mouths frozen open, scales covered with oil.

"I thought it was a curse from the devil," Doña Licha laughed, her smooth face opening to show a full mouth of white teeth. "I just stood on the shore with my three children who have families of their own and who all fish with me and we just watched the fish on the sand. It looked like a plague on my life. I cried for days. I thought we were finished. For us, fish are life. I can feel when they are biting. My heart beats faster. It's like some communication with them."

Leticia Roman, Doña Licha, remembers when the people of her area on the outskirts of Ponce, Puerto Rico's southern metropolis, walked to the shores, their pails filled with the day's shining wet catch. "The people would come around noon. We would be back already. We would go out about five o'clock in the morning in our boats, hundreds of boats covering the water like crabs on a beach. That was before the factories came."

When she said these things Doña Licha was sixty years old— an artifact of Puerto Rico's economic past, a fisherwoman who still worked at the trade which had been her family's for centuries and has run in the blood of the people of Ponce since Puerto Rico was a Spanish colony.

"My grandfather owned the largest boat in this town. It was made of wood he himself had cut as a young man. Then, you cut wood at your own risk from the trees, because the Spanish were still here and they took all the good wood to make boats themselves.

"We have black skin. We have slave blood, and even in the early 1800s when my grandfather was still a boy, there was no law against killing a slave blood. Making a boat, if you were black, was a crime. But he made his boat and went to fish.

"I never knew that kind of pain

because, when the Americans came here, things became a lot better. I never knew the Spanish, only the American soldiers who would come here to take fish from us."

Licha said these things one day in 1975. As she spoke, she scaled a fish and, without pausing, tossed it naked into a tub of ice, picked up a thick branch with the toes of one foot, and wiped the scales off her thick, sharp knife. The entire process took a half minute. After checking the blade for sharpness and adjusting the kerchief on her head, she began scaling another fish.

"The Americans always wanted the head cut off," she laughed. "It was so stupid. I would scale them well but they were boys who didn't eat much fish." She shook her head. "Such a big country and they know nothing." How much did people pay for the fish? "Two cents, sometimes three.

The people paid that," she said looking up briefly. "The Americans didn't pay anything then."

But two or three cents went quite a way back then and, while the fish were plentiful, shimmering in the clear blue waters off the coast of the island, the *pescadores*⁰ lived well. Their "industry" was Puerto Rico's most important. "All the islands live from fish," Licha said. "Island, water, fish ... obviously."

Those days are gone. "They came with their factories," she said, waving a hand toward the giant petrochemical plants in Guayanilla ten miles away. "They came to commit barbarities on the fish. They made jobs for some but they made the water too hot, the air became thick with the black smoke and the smell, the fish couldn't breathe ... they couldn't live in the hot water. Then it started, the waves of fish."

"At least there are families with men still here. The men could go to work in the factories but my man is dead. I am old and I know nothing else but catching and cleaning fish. What do I know

of oil? I thought, how will I live?"

Even though her catch has been cut down to less than a fourth of what it was, yielding her about twelve dollars a day, Doña Licha has learned how to live—she pays no rent, still living in the concrete house her father built about three-quarters of a mile up a hill outside San German, off the road which the military used to make its way around the island long ago. The house is typical of Puerto Rico's architecture, developed to cut material and labor expenses to a minimum. Her living room, the first room one encounters after walking through the always open door, is small with two steel, glassless, shuttered windows looking out onto the road. Licha keeps her color television, her most prized possession, in that room. It's always shiny and on it rest the family pictures and a drawing of the Sacred Heart which she won, two decades ago, in a church raffle. The room includes cheaply made mahogany veneered furniture, with orange patterned material protected by plastic covers. The smell of food drifts in from the kitchen, which is next to the living room,

Artist: Rini Templeton

and boasts most of the modern appliances, including stove and refrigerator, but no washing machine—Licha washes her clothes in a large washbasin.

Toward the back of the room, in an inconspicuous place almost invisible in the candle light, there is a picture of a young man, still probably a teenager with a shy smile on his face. He wears a U.S. army uniform and has written "to my beloved mother, your blessings are appreciated." The picture is framed in purple cloth. Licha Roman lost her youngest son when the army called him to fight in Korea. She was over forty when he died. "Sometimes I think that it was unfair for him to go. You see it all: they take my fish as they took my son. You ask why I am bitter?"

So each month, Doña Licha walks down the two-mile winding path from her cement home, off the area's main dirt road, to the *bodega*° of Silverio Ramírez Acosta. Don° Silverio is a creature of habit; the *plátanos*° he sells must hang from wire hangers the same way, over the same window of his store, all the time. The cans of beans and pigeon peas, which come all the way from the Goya factory in New Jersey, always occupy the same shelves. He himself has been sitting on the same wooden milk crate outside the *bodega* for as long as anyone in the area can remember. And his response to Licha's monthly visit is always the same. He sends his grandson, who helps at the store when not in school,

to get his car keys and as Licha approaches, he politely rises, removing the hat from his balding brown head, and offers the keys. "Take my car if you're going to the city," he urges.

"No. It's all right," she protests, "I can walk."

"No, no," he almost shouts, "No woman could walk to Ponce from here. Please, take my car."

After a bit more resistance, Doña Licha nods. She takes the keys and drives the Ford seven miles into Ponce, where she will stand in line with fifty or sixty other people and wait for her food stamps.

The lines wind through the government offices, snakes of sweaty, impatient people waiting to buy the key to their survival. A family of four can earn up to 300 dollars in food stamps each month; when there's little to start with, every bit counts. With that money, Leticia Roman can go to the *colmado* (grocery store) in her area and walk along the aisles that are lined with cans and bags of products made in the United States, picking and choosing what she likes.

She buys ten-pound bags of rice, which the store owner helps carry to the car. She purchases twenty cans of different varieties of beans, and meat, sauces, spices, and, finally, an assortment of vegetables. Her purchases fill eight or nine bags, which she piles in the back seat of the car, careful to put the four dozen eggs, shipped that morning from the United States, on top.

When everything is packed away, she skillfully pulls out the food stamps which correspond to the numbers on the adding machine and smiles. The food stamps have done their stuff. "I don't like to take anything from anyone," Licha says, as she leaves the store. "Especially the Americans. They send the food stamps and we eat from them." She shakes her head faintly. "But if it weren't for their factories and that smoke, I would be living from my boat and fish. So I suppose they owe me this." She shrugs. "Anyway, they benefit from the smoke; I benefit from the stamps. We end up even. That's the American way of doing things."

—Abridged from: Alfredo López, *Doña Licha's Island: Modern Colonialism in Puerto Rico* (South End Press, 1987).

Vocabulary

Doña: title of respect for a married or older woman

pescadores: fishermen

bodega: small grocery store

Don: title of respect for a man

plátano: vegetable resembling a large banana (plantain)

READING
We can't stand more toxic wastes in the air ...

INTERVIEW WITH PURITA GIL PÉREZ

I've been living in this community for about 12 years. At the moment, I'm living on a street right across from the pipes that lead from the Du Pont factory to the waste treatment plant in Barceloneta⁰. All of us who live in this area are suffering lung problems, breathing problems, allergies and itchy eyes.

It appears that there are leaks. Sometimes you can tell there's been a leak because of the bad odor. This happens mainly at night. It seems that the gas escapes from the joints in the pipes, or from the drain.

A number of communities close to the Du Pont factory are affected. Cantito, where I live, is the community farthest from the factory, but nearest to the piping.

Of course, it's not Du Pont alone. This north coast area is completely contaminated, it's overloaded with toxic wastes from all the pharmaceutical plants⁰ in the area. We oppose the manufacture of herbicide⁰ here for precisely that reason, because we are already so affected and can't stand more toxic waste in the air.

What are the main problems that the herbicide plant would bring?

First of all, there is the danger of leaks. The manufacture of

Air pollution from a south coast oil refinery.

herbicide uses a substance which specialists have told us is highly toxic, caustic. It's first-cousin to the substance that escaped from the plant in Bhopal, India. Once it leaks out, it would produce vomiting and coughing, with a corrosive effect on the lungs. It could cause death.

The plant would also affect the water around Manatí. The

company wants to use an additional 100 thousand gallons of water per day from the Tortuguera Lagoon. This will lower the water level of the lagoon so that salty ocean water flows in, changing the ecological balance.

The people in Barceloneta are firmly opposed to receiving more liquid waste, because the waste treatment plant there is obsolete and already over-loaded.

What has been the community's response?

First, the mayor got together with some of his cronies and formed a committee to stop Du Pont. It was basically a form of extortion, to get Du Pont to give money to the town. As soon as Du Pont offered them $250,000 as payment for certain licenses, the mayor's group disbanded.

Some members of the group got angry about this sell-out. Others in the community were furious too, so we formed a new group known as the Manatí Environmental Committee. The Committee visited families, gave out information, and spoke out against Du Pont and the mayor. It gained members and broad sympathy, and managed to arrange for public hearings to be held.

More than 1,300 people came to the hearings, including representatives from Du Pont, from the government's Environmental Quality Board, and members of the community. The Du Pont representatives were very arrogant. Once they had given their speech—in which they said the company has plants in the U.S. and Australia and has never had any problems—they refused to listen to any of us. They got up one by one, without even saying

goodnight, and left the room.

We're trying to raise the awareness of the community. We have working with us an allergist, Dr. Figueroa, who treated me when I suffered a respiratory arrest due to the gas leaks. He's amazed at how his office is always full of people suffering from respiratory ailments. In May we organized a talk in which he told us about the health dangers of pollution.

The Committee has done these things with very little money. You can't compare us with Du Pont, which is spending tens of thousands of dollars on advertising. They've had to spend a fortune to convince the people of Manatí and of Puerto Rico that they are keeping the water clean and that they provide a lot of jobs, which isn't true.

How many people in this community work for Du Pont?

Only four or five. There's a false idea that we should toler-ate the pollution of all these factories because "this is progress." It's not so. The factories which locate in Puerto Rico cause a lot of toxic pollu-tion but they employ very few people.

The government believes that Du Pont will bring jobs to the community, but we do not. This kind of work is highly technical. We predict that they won't employ anyone from our com-munity, since most people here don't have technical training. But we're the ones running the health risk.

We're not opposed to progress. We want Du Pont, which has already spent so much on advertising, to send technicians who can find out what is happening. If they really care about the community, they should carry out an investigation into how our health is, how the pipes are and the whole situation.

What about you, why did you get involved in this?

I got involved because I've got a social conscience.   In 1976 I took part in a campaign to stop Du Pont from dumping toxic waste in the Manatí River. The fish in the river were dying, the fishermen protested and we supported them.   We held public hearings and pickets, but we didn't win.

I supported the fishermen because it seemed to me unjust that they were taking away the means of making a living from these humble people. Now I'm getting involved in this fight, first of all because I'm sick myself, secondly because when I go to the clinic I see sick children who can't breathe. I'm also worried about the possibility of a major escape of gas, as has happened elsewhere in Puerto Rico recently.

I believe we're doing something good. I hope our struggle won't be in vain, that we'll some day have better air for our lungs, so we can breathe freely. It will be a victory for poor people, for those whose voices are not heard.

–Abridged from: Interview with Purita Gil Pérez, in *De Prisa* (published by National Ecumenical Movement of Puerto Rico, PRISA), August 1986.

Note: The editors requested materials from the DuPont Co. regarding their program in Puerto Rico to be included in this packet. At publication time, however, these had not been received.

Vocabulary

Barceloneta: industrial town on Puerto Rico's north coast

pharmaceutical plants: factories manufacturing drugs for medical use

herbicide: chemical used to kill vegetation

TEACHER GUIDE
Vieques and the Navy

▶ **OBJECTIVES**

Students will:

1. Compare and contrast the views of the people of Vieques and the U.S. Navy about the Navy's use of Vieques

2. Describe the process by which the U.S. Navy acquired land on Vieques and its impact on the lives of the islanders

3. Evaluate the protests by Vieques fishermen—justified acts of civil disobedience, or criminal wrongdoing?

▶ **QUESTIONS FOR DISCUSSION**

1. When and how did the U.S. Navy acquire land on Vieques?

What does the Navy do there? Why?

2. Why did many residents of Vieques leave? How did Navy's presence affect the people who remained on the island?

3. Imagine that a foreign government has purchased land not far from where you live in order to practice bombing there. How would you feel? What might you do, if anything?

4. How have Viequens protested the Navy's presence? Do you think they were justified in their actions, or not? Explain your answer.

5. How do you think the issue should be resolved?

▶ **SUGGESTED ACTIVITIES**

1. Students locate the United States, Puerto Rico, Vieques and St. Croix on a map.

2. The class debates the following question: "The residents of Vieques were justified in blocking U.S. Navy operations in order to protest the Navy's presence. Yes or no?" Break into three teams for the debate, representing:

  a) a Vieques fishermen's group

  b) the U.S. Navy

  c) Puerto Rican government officials

Students may wish to do more research on the issue by writing to the sources listed below (see Resources).

3. Students find out about other U.S. military installations in Puerto Rico. What functions do they perform? How do Puerto Ricans feel about them?

▶ **RESOURCES**

1. Two organizations which can provide information on U.S. military activities in Puerto Rico, from an anti-militarism perspective:

- Caribbean Project for Justice & Peace, P.O. Box 21226, Río Piedras, PR 00928. (809) 763-2451

- PRISA, Apt. 2448, Bayamón, PR 00619. (809) 787-7274

2. For information about Vieques activities from the U.S. Navy's point of view, students may write to: Commander, Fleet Air Caribbean, U.S. Naval Station, Attention: Public Affairs Officer, Box 3037, FPO Miami, FL 34051-8000.

INTRODUCTION
Vieques and the Navy

The small island of Vieques sits six miles off Puerto Rico's east coast. During World War Two, the U.S. Navy acquired 26,000 of the island's 33,000 acres of land. Some large landowners sold willingly, but many tenant farmers and share-croppers, who farmed land not their own, were forcibly evicted from their homes. The Navy built military bases on the east and west ends of Vieques, leaving a small strip in the center for the island's people.

Construction of the bases initially employed some Viequens. But when it was completed, the jobs dried up. With most of the island's farm-land and fishing waters off-limits, Vieques people found it hard to make a living.

People began leaving: migrating to the United States, to the main island of Puerto Rico, and to nearby St. Croix, in the U.S. Virgin Islands. About 10,000 people had lived on Vieques before the Navy came; by 1960, only about 7,000 remained. Severino Rivera Morales, a Vieques resident, remembers how it was when the Navy arrived.

Vieques became part of the U.S. Navy's Atlantic Fleet Weapons Range. The bases included areas for combat training, an artillery firing range, and targets for dropping live bombs.

The shelling of Vieques with live ammunition was particularly disruptive to fishermen. It destroyed their nets and traps, and kept them out of the best fishing grounds. Angel Ventura Cintrón, a fisherman, describes the impact on the islanders' lives.

In 1978, a group of Vieques fishermen organized the first major protest against the Navy presence. Warships from the United States, Canada, Britain and other western nations were preparing for joint naval exer-cises. These were to include surface shooting, missile

Amphibious landing by U.S. naval forces on Vieques during 1981 maneuvers code-named "Ocean Venture '81."

launching and other war maneuvers. As the exercises were about to begin, forty small fishing boats sailed into the warships' path.

The maneuvers were delayed, and five fishermen were arrested. Charges were later dropped.The next year, the fishermen again delayed the start of a two-week long series of war games. The Navy had to halt ship-to-shore firing for several hours after 20 small boats of the Vieques Fishermen's Association lined up along the firing range. A 437-foot U.S. guided missile destroyer fired twelve volleys over the protesters' boats before the exercise was suspended. But when the fishermen headed back to shore, firing resumed.

The fishermen's committee eventually disbanded. But in 1989, protest flared again, this time in the form of a squatters' movement demanding access to land.

The Navy argues that Vieques is needed for training U.S. military forces, and is essential to national security. But some Viequens do not agree that they should be the ones to give up their land and livelihood. Says Severino Rivera Morales: "It has been this little bit of earth which has contributed most in all the world to that which the American knows as national defense."

READING

The History of Vieques and the Navy Is a Long One ...

INTERVIEW WITH SEVERINO RIVERA MORALES

The history of Vieques and the Navy is a long one, from way back. At the time the Navy came here, the people themselves didn't know how it came about. The things that happened at the time of the Navy's arrival are somewhat dramatic situations which can be called unjust ...

The Navy originally established a base. This involved a series of expropriations°. There were some large landowners who negotiated the sale of their lands; there were others who were simply obliged to abandon them. The population was removed from those places by orders, practically at gunpoint, and was moved to other areas obtained for them, which were called "wards."

Many families came to live in those wards, where there was neither water, electricity, streets, nor any kind of housing. At that time, they had only a little termite-ridden lumber and a few sheets of zinc°. It was of little concern to the Navy if it were day or night when these forced expropriations were carried out. The only thing they gave the people was a short letter in which they were told that possibly they could be evicted again with 24 hours' notice, in which case they would not be assigned further land for living sites.

Later, a few jobs were created on the base and some Viequens were employed. That naturally was like the times of old prospecting and the gold rush, and many people forgot about the kinds of things which had been done to them.

Once the Americans decided to cut back personnel on the base, practically the whole population was left without means of support. They were left almost without land for the development of agriculture and cattle raising, and without other economic resources such as fishing, in the area where the base was established on the western side.

Then, the expropriations on the east were carried out. This base was to be one entirely for military practices of bombing and shelling, physical training for Marines, etc. The families of the east were moved to the ward which the Puerto Rican government obtained for them, called Tortuguero. There was some old housing left from a camp, and some termite-eaten lumber. They were dumped there without work and without a clear way of surviving.

As a result of this there came about emigration to other countries in search of sources of income. Tragedy and suffering accompanied these experiences of emigration; the destruction of marriages and families because husbands and fathers left, looking for work ...

It has been this little bit of earth which has contributed most in all the world to that which the American knows as national defense ...

—Abridged from: *Vieques and Christians*, published by the National Ecumenical Movement of Puerto Rico (PRISA), 1981.

Vocabulary

expropriation: the taking of private property, usually by a government agency, sometimes in exchange for compensation

zinc: corrugated iron sheets used for roofing

READING
The Whole People of Vieques Has Suffered...

INTERVIEW WITH ANGEL VENTURA CINTRÓN

I had a lot of problems with the United States Navy, because at that time they didn't take the fishermen into consideration. They didn't distribute lists of firing schedules, neither the time nor the place nor anything. I took my 11-year-old son spearfishing at depths of 30, 40, 50 feet ... I had to do it to subsist. For me the Navy was a permanent obstacle, because when we most needed to earn a living, they expelled us under fire. Even though the pilots of the airplanes and ships saw us, they fired.

I remember that on one occasion, we were in Salinas, trying to catch a lobster that was being difficult. Two planes came flying in to fire and they shot directly at the small boat where we were. Four bullets struck at our right, four to the left, and one ricocheted off, with the sound of a 50-caliber machine gun. We had to leave everything and go home without fish and with a tremendous scare.

We complained to the "Gray Empire" by telephone, because at that time they didn't allow anybody in up there [at the military base] but the good-looking, the intellectuals, teachers, the judge, the mayor, and other people of wealth. Those were the only ones who entered the base at the time I'm telling you about. If you arrived at the gate to ask for a pass, they said in English, "I'm sorry." That's all they said there. "I'm sorry. You can't enter."

They used to wake us up at 4:30 or 5:00 a.m., flying at an altitude of about 100 feet. On one occasion, I had worked all day and had gone to sleep very tired, but one of my boys had an earache. From about 8:00 p.m. I was with that baby, rocking him in my arms, giving him ear-drops and doing a thousand things more or less helplessly. My wife rocked him while I tried to sleep, because I had to get up at 4:00 a.m. to go to work.

When I had that boy almost asleep, when sleep was getting the better of the pain, I thought, "Blessed be God, at least it's only 3:00 a.m. and I can get an hour's sleep." Then there came the jets flying low, right over the house, firing those cannons and the baby turning over and jumped up.

So then instead of going to work, I had to stay up with the baby and go to the hospital with him, because the pain not only increased, he also had a nervous attack that I thought would kill him. And there were other such cases, not only with me; the whole people of Vieques has suffered from them.

Right now, I can say that with the battles we've brought against the Navy, the matters of early morning firing and of low-flying jet airplanes have lessened a little.

—Abridged from: *Vieques and Christians,* published by the National Ecumenical Movement of Puerto Rico (PRISA), 1981.

READING
Vieques Island Dwellers Take Over Navy Land
Residents Live Surrounded by 'No-Trespassing' Signs

BY WILLIAM STEIF

Vieques, Puerto Rico (LP)

Between 200 and 400 well-organized squatters° have moved onto land owned by the United States Navy on this 18-mile long island off the east coast of Puerto Rico.

Vieques, part of the U.S. Commonwealth of Puerto Rico, is almost mid-way between Puerto Rico and the U.S. Virgin Islands. For decades, it has been a bombing and target practice range for U.S. Navy ships on Caribbean maneuvers.

The island is approximately 33,000 acres. Of these, the U.S. Navy owns 26,000 acres, most of it acquired in 1940.

Vieques' 8,000 residents live near the island's western end on a small tract of land surrounded by barbed wire fences and signs indicating that everything beyond the fences is restricted land on which trespassing is prohibited.

The Navy presence has had a dramatic impact on the island. Daily life is constantly interrupted by the sounds of explosions, planes and target practice.

"My grandchild nervously runs every time he hears a plane. A neighbor's child, who is 2, trembles whenever he hears a loud noise. These are the psychological effects. Another child has been mute since an explosion," commented one island resident.

Moreover, island residents have practically no land at their disposal. Farming has all but disappeared and fishing is limited to a few specific areas. Within these limitations agricultural and urban development have been impossible.

Housing shortages are a major problem for Vieques residents on an island where land and home prices have soared 400 to 600 percent in the last decade. Aside from the lack of land, the rising prices are caused by buying pressure exerted by wealthy Puerto Ricans. Most of them, from the capital city of San Juan, come to Vieques seeking beach retreats.

The land takeover followed an April 14 incident in which about 100 Vieques residents burned two Navy trucks during a clash with sailors and U.S. marshals who were trying to evict a squatter from Navy land.

Carlos Zenón, a squatter leader, called the late May takeover a "land rescue." The seizure was organized by the Vieques Association for Home Ownership, headed by Antonio Figueroa.

The association squatters moved onto an 880-acre called La Hueca, or The Hollow, on the island's dusty western end. The whole 880 acres is Navy-owned

Carlos Zenón

but the squatters occupied only 100 acres and immediately started to cut roads, chop down trees, measure off plots and put up huts bearing family names.

Figueroa said his association had at least 200 applications for housing and that the association is only seeking to reclaim land sold to the Navy in 1940.

Meanwhile, from their main base at Roosevelt Roads in

southeastern Puerto Rico, Navy spokespersons said the Navy was looking for "legal avenues" to evict the squatters.

Vieques has had a long history of struggle against the Navy. In the late 1970s, the Crusade for the Rescue of Vieques and the Vieques Fishermen's Association were created. Their activities have included organized protests and the obstruction of bombing maneuvers.

The Navy's response has been to retaliate. For example, in 1979, 21 people were arrested and sentenced to maximum jail terms, a stiff penalty for trespassing.

In another incident, fishermen brought a civil suit against the Navy for the destruction of fishing traps, but the case was transferred to the U.S., making it impossible for the fishermen to attend.

In the 1960s, the Navy was not only using Vieques but also Culebra, a smaller Puerto Rican island close to St. Thomas, for target practice. Protests from a few hundred residents there had more success than similar protests from the residents of Vieques. Culebra finally shut the Navy out of the island and has since become a haven for yacht operators.

Some Vieques residents say that the most likely resolution of the latest land takeover will be for the Navy to transfer some of its land to the Commonwealth, presumably for distribution to Vieques residents.

The Commonwealth is the island's second largest landowner, with just over 4,000 acres. Vieques' Mayor Santiago Collazo has asked the Commonwealth to transfer 1,800 acres to the municipality but he has had no response so far.

–Reprinted from: *Latinamerica Press*, June 22, 1989.

Vocabulary

squatters: people who move onto vacant lands for the purpose of living or farming

READING
The Navy Replies to Critics

Department of the Navy
Office of the Chief of Naval Operations
Washington, D.C. 20350

"The strategic importance of Vieques is mainly in its geographic location and the prepositioned ammunition stocks needed in support of Navy and Marine Corps deployed units. If the use of the Vieques Ammunition Facility were denied, logistic flexibility to support operational units would be unacceptably restricted.

Further, the island of Vieques is used to support training of the Atlantic Fleet. It is the only adequate naval gunfire range on the Atlantic coast. A portion of the Naval Ammunition Facility is used by the U.S. Marines as a maneuver area which is important during larger training maneuvers, and it also provides a variation in terrain and vegetation not available at other eastern maneuver areas. It is the only facility available on the east coast for year round operations where extensive naval gunfire support can be provided for the maneuvers.

Because Vieques is a part of a larger training and operating complex in the Caribbean there are no known documents which specifically define Vieques as 'vital'. Nevertheless, it is our opinion that the continued use of Vieques is vital to national security."

—Vice Admiral T.J. Bigley, Office of the Chief of Naval Operations, Department of the Navy, letter in response to Freedom of Information Act request, Sept. 12, 1978.

"We need to stay here in the Caribbean and continue our training. Vieques is a key part of our operation. If you want national defense you have to keep the Navy strong. Only if the Navy is strong will we be able to protect you."

—Rear Admiral Arthur Knoizen, former commander of U.S. forces in the Caribbean, quoted in *The St. Croix Avis*, Jan. 18, 1979.

"We need to stay here in the Caribbean and continue our training. Vieques is a key part of our operation. If you want national defense you have to keep the Navy strong. Only if the Navy is strong will we be able to protect you."

—Rear Admiral Arthur Knoizen

TEACHER GUIDE
What Future for Puerto Rico?

▶ **OBJECTIVES**

Students will:

1. List pivotal events in Puerto Rico's historical relationship with the United States

2. Evaluate pros and cons for each of Puerto Rico's three status options

3. Predict possible consequences of each option for both Puerto Rico and the United States

▶ **QUESTIONS FOR DISCUSSION**

1. When did the relationship between Puerto Rico and the United States begin? How has it changed over time? (Refer for more information to "A Brief History of Puerto Rico.")

2. What is a colony? Some people say that the relationship of Puerto Rico to the U.S. is a colonial one. Do you agree? Why or why not?

▶ **SUGGESTED ACTIVITIES**

1. Three students present and debate the alternative positions regarding Puerto Rico's status. Encourage them to do additional research on the issues. The rest of class will take notes and ask questions during the debate, then write short position papers based on the debate and the readings.

▶ **RESOURCES**

1. An article addressing all sides of the status debate is "Prisoners of Many Myths: Puerto Rico's Future Status," by Antonio Stevens-Arroyo, in *The Nation*, January 22, 1990.

2. The Congressional Research Service of the Library of Congress offers an issue brief entitled "Puerto Rico: Political Status Options" by Bette A. Taylor, Jan. 5, 1990. Order code IB89065.

3. *Puerto Rico: Our Right to Decide* is a 30-minute film presenting Puerto Ricans' diverse views on the status question. Includes interviews with students, teachers, farmers, fishermen and others. 16 mm or VHS. Available from the Centro de Estudios Puertorriqueños.

4. The following books are suitable for senior high and above:

• Raymond Carr, *Puerto Rico: A Colonial Experiment* (New York University Press, 1984). Generally pro-statehood perspective.

• L.L. Cripps, *Puerto Rico: The Case for Independence* (Schenkman Pub. Co., 1974). In favor of independence and socialism.

INTRODUCTION
What Future for Puerto Rico?

Puerto Rico's relationship with the United States under the "Commonwealth" system is unique. Puerto Ricans are U.S. citizens. They can be drafted into the U.S. military; hundreds have died fighting for the U.S. in overseas wars. They vote in presidential primaries, but cannot vote in presidential elections unless they live on the U.S. mainland.

The U.S. Congress controls many aspects of Puerto Rican affairs. It decides which federal laws apply to the island. Yet Puerto Rico's delegate in Congress, called the Resident Commissioner, can vote only in committee and not on the floor of the House of Representatives.

This relationship has been controversial ever since the United States assumed control of Puerto Rico in 1898. Many countries have criticized the United States for continuing to hold a "colony." In Puerto Rico, debate over the status issue is continuous. Islanders are divided between those who favor the present Commonwealth arrangement, those who would prefer Puerto Rico to become a U.S. state, and those who wish it to be an independent country.

The issues are complex. Under the present arrangement, U.S. companies which invest in Puerto Rico are exempt from paying taxes on the profits they earn there. If Puerto Rico became a state, this special arrangement presumably would cease, and investors might withdraw. The U.S. federal government spends $6 billion per year on Puerto Rico, including welfare and food stamps, development aid, and the salaries of federal employees. Backers of Commonwealth status argue that Puerto Ricans' living standards would fall if these subsidies ended, as presumably would happen under independence.

Statehood advocates argue that the island would have more prestige and rights as a U.S. state, including full Congressional representation and a wider range of federal grants and welfare benefits. They say statehood would attract more U.S. investors and tourists, resulting in an economic boom.

Backers of independence contend that Puerto Rico's colonial relationship with the United States is the root cause of the island's problems. These include high unemployment, welfare dependency, drug abuse and pollution. Puerto Ricans can only build a healthy society and maintain their culture, they believe, if they become independent.

The issue of culture and language is an important one. Virtually everyone in Puerto Rico speaks Spanish; only about 20 percent also speak English fluently. Most Puerto Ricans feel strongly that the use of Spanish must continue. But the U.S. Congress may be unwilling to accept Puerto Rico as a state if it does not agree to use English for government, business and education.

Within the next few years, Puerto Ricans may vote in a plebiscite on what the island's future status should be. The following statements present arguments in favor of each of the three alternatives.

READING
We Need Statehood to Have Full Political Power

INTERVIEW WITH BALTASAR CORRADA DEL RÍO, FORMER RESIDENT COMMISSIONER, COMMONWEALTH OF PUERTO RICO

How would you assess Puerto Rico's current relationship with the United States?

The relationship between Puerto Rico and the United States, of course, is very close. We, Puerto Ricans, are citizens of the United States. The economic, social, and political integration between Puerto Rico and the U.S. is great. Out of five million Puerto Ricans, three million reside on the island of Puerto Rico and over two million reside on the U.S. mainland. Therefore, a tremendous degree of social interaction takes place between residents of the island and the mainland. The eco-nomic relationship is also very close because many large American companies have investments in Puerto Rico.

What would independence mean for Puerto Rico?

It would mean, first of all, that Puerto Ricans would not have freedom to move back and forth between the island of Puerto Rico and the U.S. mainland as we now have because we are citizens of the United States. Puerto Ricans would be subject to U.S. immigration laws.

Secondly, the industrializa-tion of Puerto Rico and its economic development of the last 30 years has been based mainly on American companies doing business in Puerto Rico, investing there, and creating jobs. We believe that inde-pendence would bring a large degree of uncertainty about the investment of capital by Ameri-can businesses in Puerto Rico which would result in a terrible exacerbation of our problems of unemployment and certainly a greater poverty.

What would be the consequences of statehood?

The fact that we are in a kind of political limbo, neither a state of the union, nor an independent state, works against the better opportunities

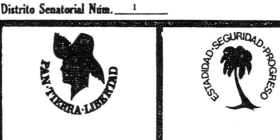

MODELO
ELECCIONES GENERALES

TRIBUNAL ELECTORAL DE PUERTO RICO

PAPELETA ELECTORAL

Municipio de ___SAN JUAN___

Distrito Senatorial Núm. ___1___

PARTIDO POPULAR DEMOCRATICO | PARTIDO NUEVO PROGRESISTA | PARTIDO INDEPENDENTISTA PUERTORRIQUEÑO | PARTIDO SOCIALISTA PUERTORRIQUEÑO

Sample ballot in the 1976 election, showing symbols of the electoral parties. The Popular Demo-cratic Party favors the Commonwealth system; the New Progressive Party seeks statehood; and the Puerto Rican Independence Party and Puerto Rican Socialist Party advocate independence.

of the Puerto Ricans.   We need statehood to have full political power.   The vast majority of Puerto Ricans want to retain their American citizenship; we are entitled to all the rights and responsibilities of that citizenship.

Statehood is independence in the sense that we would form part of an independent nation, the United States of America. We would be able to retain our identity as a people by insisting when we petition Congress for statehood that our cultural heritage, our Spanish language, and our identity as a Latin American people would have to be respected.

If a referendum on the status issue were held, what outcome would you predict?

There are some who believe that if we had a plebiscite between statehood and independence and the current Commonwealth status, the result might be 80 percent for statehood and about 20 percent for independence. Under the best circumstances, independence would not carry more than 20 percent of the vote.

Our people are now realizing that as a U.S. territory or possession, we are second-class American citizens and that we are in a political limbo. We need the dignity that statehood would bring about. At the same time, we are instilling in our people the confidence that we do not have to assimilate to an Anglo-Saxon[0] culture and that we can continue to be what we are—ethnically, racially, and culturally.

—Abridged from: *Transafrica Forum*, November 1982.

Vocabulary

Anglo-Saxon: of the English-speaking, northern European cultural tradition

READING
Commonwealth Status Represents a Breakthrough

INTERVIEW WITH JAIME B. FUSTER, RESIDENT COMMISSIONER OF PUERTO RICO IN THE U.S. HOUSE OF REPRESENTATIVES

How would you assess Puerto Rico's current relationship with the United States?

Puerto Rico has chosen free association with the United States as an "Estado Libre Asociado" within the U.S. federal system. As a Commonwealth, Puerto Rico exercises large control over its internal affairs. We recognize the pre-eminence of the U.S. federal government in defense, foreign affairs, currency and other such areas.

The result today is one of dramatic success. Puerto Rico, formerly one of the most impoverished places in the hemisphere, now has a dynamic, growing economy. Its per-capita income tops that of any Latin American country. Since 1940, life expectancy has jumped from 46 years to 73.6 years, one of the highest in the world. The island's exports have risen dramatically from $221 million in 1940 to $12 billion in 1987.

American corporations and individuals have invested over $20 billion in Puerto Rico, from which they realize substantial profits while simultaneously creating jobs and income in Puerto Rico.

What would independence mean for Puerto Rico?

Independence would mean

"Bread, Land, Liberty"—slogan of the Popular Democratic Party, which favors Commonwealth status

the loss of many of the economic conditions that Puerto Rico needs to achieve full prosperity. These include total free access to the U.S. market, a ready source of development capital, and unrestricted access to the U.S. workforce and education centers.

Close ties with the U.S. are necessary in order to cope with the economic problems of a densely populated island with almost no resources, and in order to provide a decent standard of living for our people.

What would be the consequences of statehood?

Statehood implies economic risks and burdens. Under Commonwealth, Puerto Ricans tax themselves for running their government, but are not subject to federal income taxes. Under statehood, Puerto Ricans would have to pay federal taxes. By definition, as a state, Puerto Rico would also lose the tax-exemption benefits given to mainland corporations that locate in Puerto Rico under Section 936 of the Internal Revenue Code.

As powerful as the American influence has been in Puerto Rico, we still adhere to the Spanish language. Our traditions differ from those of the mainland, and we want to preserve this distinct cultural personality. Many of us in Puerto Rico fear that statehood would eventually mean the island's cultural absorption by the mainland, as happened with Louisiana, New Mexico and Hawaii.

If a referendum on the status issue were held, what outcome would you predict?

I predict a majority in favor of Commonwealth. To us, Commonwealth status, even with its imperfections, represents a breakthrough. Both independence and statehood conflict with vital Puerto Rican aspirations.

But the present arrangement has a flaw, in that the U.S. Congress has unilateral authority to apply federal laws to Puerto Rico. We prefer an "enhanced" Commonwealth status, in which we in Puerto Rico would have a role in determining when federal laws apply to the island.

–Abridged from: Statement by Jaime B. Fuster, Senate Energy Committee, San Juan Hearings, June 16, 1989; and "Puerto Rican Democratic Development," entered into the Congressional Record by Jaime B. Fuster, March 31, 1988.

Vocabulary

Estado Libre Asociado: Associated Free State, the legal term for Puerto Rico's Commonwealth status

Section 936 of the Internal Revenue Code: provides that U.S. companies which invest in Puerto Rico do not have to pay taxes on profits earned there

READING
The Puerto Rican People Feel Puerto Rican—Not North American

INTERVIEW WITH WILMA REVERÓN-TÍO, FORMER EXECUTIVE DIRECTOR, INTERNATIONAL INFORMATION OFFICE FOR PUERTO RICAN INDEPENDENCE

How would you assess Puerto Rico's current relationship with the United States?

It is a colonial relationship. Basically, it means that the sovereignty of the people of

Puerto Rico resides in the Congress of the United States and not in Puerto Rico itself. The Congress has power to overrule or to veto legislation that has been approved by the people of Puerto Rico. We don't have any powers in terms of deciding on migration, on the airspace of Puerto Rico, or on the coastal waters.

What would independence mean for Puerto Rico?

Independence would mean that we could determine what kind of relationship we would have with the U.S. We would hope that we could establish a friendly and respectful relationship in which the U.S. would respect our right to decide [on our affairs], and we would respect their right to decide on national policy. We would decide what kind of government we wanted and with whom we were going to have relationships.

The unemployment and the utter dependency the people of Puerto Rico have on the United States' federal assistance is proof that the current colonial relationship is not working.

Our economy has been structured in a way to insure that we are going to be dependent all the time. Our industry has been geared and oriented toward what the U.S. market needs and not toward the needs of the people of Puerto Rico. We import 80 percent of what we consume and that basically means that we do not produce anything that we need.   So, when we produce, it is not for us at all.

The only answer is for Puerto Ricans to have the right to decide what economic policy decisions should be made for Puerto Rico. The people of Puerto Rico now have the resources, the skills, and the know-how to administer their own economy and their own industry.

What would be the consequences of statehood?

The Puerto Rican people feel overwhelmingly Puerto Rican—not North American. We have an Hispanic culture; we speak Spanish; we have different music from U.S. people; we have our own literature and our own poetry, which is very rich and creative. There would be great cultural resistance to being annexed to an Anglo-Saxon country.

But our culture is being threatened daily. Until the establishment of the Commonwealth in 1952, education in Puerto Rico was conducted in

Photo: Juan Ibáñez

English because the U.S. imposed English as the teaching language in Puerto Rico. It was very funny because most of the teachers didn't know any English. Imagine the teachers, not knowing any English, teaching others who didn't understand English.

No one believes that the U.S. will admit a Spanish-speaking state to the Union. There is no place for that in the United States.

If a referendum on the status issue were held, what outcome would you predict?

What you have in Puerto Rico is complete dissatisfaction with the current state of affairs in Puerto Rico and complete dissatisfaction with the present relationship with the U.S. In no way, however, do I think that the people of Puerto Rico support statehood.

Only two things now are clear. First, the Puerto Rican people don't want statehood. Second, they are completely unsure about what relationship they want with the United States. That would be the result of a referendum held today.

–Abridged from: *TransAfrica Forum*, November 1982.

Sources of Classroom Materials

▶ **PUBLISHERS AND DISTRIBUTORS**

Africa World Press, 15 Industry Court, Trenton, NJ 08638. (609) 771-1666. Non-fiction.

Caribbean Books, Box H, Parkersburg, IA 50665. (319) 346-2048. Distributes a wide variety of books on the Caribbean, including many hard to find elsewhere. (As of 1990, they were clearing out their inventory at a discount.)

Heinemann, 70 Court St., Portsmouth, NH 03801. (603) 431-7894. Fiction and non-fiction.

Longman Group Ltd., Longman House, Burnt Mill, Harlow, Essex, CM20 2JE, England. Telephone: (0279) 26721. Fiction and non-fiction. Publishes *Caribbean Story*, a two-volume illustrated history of the Caribbean for secondary schools.

Monthly Review Press, 155 West 23 St., New York, NY 10011. (212) 691-2555. Non-fiction. Also distributes books published by the Latin America Bureau in London, including short profiles of several Caribbean countries.

South End Press, 116 St. Botolph St., Boston, MA 02115. (617) 266-0629. Non-fiction.

Thomas Nelson & Sons. Ltd., Nelson House, Mayfield Road, Walton-on-Thames, Surrey KT12 5PL, England. Telephone: (0932) 246133. Publishes *The Caribbean People*, a three-volume illustrated history of the Caribbean appropriate for middle school students.

Three Continents Press, 1901 Pennsylvania Ave. N.W., Washington, DC 20006. (202) 223-2554. Fiction.

Zed Books, 171 First Avenue, Atlantic Highlands, NJ 07716. Non-fiction.

▶ **FILMS**

Centro de Estudios Puertorriqueños, Hunter College, 695 Park Avenue, New York, NY 10021. (212) 772-5689.

Cinema Guild, 1697 Broadway, New York, NY 10019. (212) 246-5522.

New Yorker Films, 16 West 61 St., New York, NY 10023.

New Day Films, 853 Broadway #1210, New York, NY 10003.

▶ **ORGANIZATIONS**

Ecumenical Program on Central America and the Caribbean (EPICA)
1470 Irving St., N.W.
Washington, DC 20010
(202) 332-0292

Casa de la Herencia Cultural Puertorriqueña
1 East 104 St., Room 458
New York, NY 10029
(212) 722-2600

Centro de Estudios Puertorriqueños
Hunter College
695 Park Avenue
New York, NY 10021
(212) 772-5689

National Congress for Puerto Rican Rights
160 West Lippincott
Philadelphia, PA 19133

National Puerto Rican Coalition
1700 K St. N.W.
Washington, DC 20006
(202) 223-3915

Policy Alternatives for the Caribbean and Central America (PACCA)
1506 19th St., N.W., Suite 2
Washington, DC 20036
(202) 332-6333

Proyecto Caribeño de Justicia y Paz
(Caribbean Project for Justice and Peace)
P.O. Box 21226
Río Piedras, PR 00928
(809) 763-2451

Puerto Rico Federal Affairs Administration
734 15th St. NW, Suite 700
Washington DC 20005
(202) 383-1300

Puerto Rico Industrial Mission
P.O. Box 3728
San Juan, PR 00936
(809) 765-4303

Taller Puertorriqueno
2721 North 5th St.
Philadelphia, PA 19133
(215) 426-3311

About the Publishers

Ecumenical Program on Central America and the Caribbean (EPICA)

Founded in 1968, EPICA educates the U.S. public about the roots of contemporary problems in the Caribbean and Central America. An independent organization working alongside the institutional church, EPICA advocates a joint strategy of change by people in the North and South of the Americas. Through grassroots public education, EPICA serves diverse constituencies working toward a new relationship with the people of the hemisphere. *Programs include*:

• A small press which publishes titles in English and Spanish on the history, politics and culture of Central American and Caribbean countries. *The Caribbean: Survival, Struggle and Sovereignty* (1988) is a comprehensive introduction to the region which is widely used as a college text.

• Workshops, seminars and speaking tours on current issues related to U.S. policies in the region. Workshops emphasize participatory learning and critical reflection in small groups.

• Study tours to Central America and the Caribbean for church and community groups. Groups have visited Haiti, Jamaica, the Dominican Republic and Puerto Rico, as well as all the Central American nations.

• The North-South Encounter workshop series, which brings lay pastoral workers from Central America to the U.S. to dialogue with people of faith in a community workshop setting.

• *Challenge*, a journal of faith writings by Central American theologians, pastoral workers and social activists.

Information center and library open to the public.

A non-profit, tax-exempt organization, EPICA is supported by the sale of publications and grants from foundations and religious bodies.

EPICA • 1470 Irving Street, NW
Washington, DC 20010 • (202) 332-0292

Network of Educators on the Americas (NECA)
(formerly the Network of Educators' Committees on Central America)

NECA is an organization of K-12 teachers, parents, students, university staff, social workers, and concerned members of the community. It works with schools to develop and promote pedagogies, resources and cross-cultural understanding for teaching about the Americas. Working with six affiliates across the country, NECA promotes critical, anti-racist, and multicultural education as a way of furthering social and economic justice in the hemisphere. *Programs include*:

• Developing and disseminating classroom resources, including books, slide shows and teaching guides, for elementary and secondary schools. Recent publications include *Rediscovering America: a bilingual anthology for teaching about the conquest and its legacy*, and *Inside the Volcano: A Curriculum on Nicaragua*. Catalogue available.

• Courses and workshops in the historical, economic, social and cultural traditions of the Americas, as well as workshops on critical teaching for K-12 teachers.

• Quarterly newsletter with reviews, classroom readings, and activities.

• Study tours for educators to El Salvador and Mexico. Participants learn about the education system in the respective countries through school visits and discussions with teachers, students, families and education officials.

• The Books Project, jointly coordinated with the George Washington University. The project provides training and support to teachers in language diverse schools who want to incorporate a process-based approach to reading and writing instruction.

A non-profit, tax-exempt organization, NECA is supported by the sale of publications and grants from foundations.

NECA • 1118 22nd Street, NW
Washington, DC 20037 • (202) 429-0137

Caribbean Connections Series

Caribbean Connections:
OVERVIEW OF REGIONAL HISTORY

❝This book's readings and activities invite students to explore Caribbean history from the inside. It joins the personal and social to tell a powerful story. I wish I'd had this curriculum when I started teaching.❞

— William Bigelow
Social Studies Teacher, Portland Public Schools
Co-editor, Rethinking Columbus

Highlights of OVERVIEW OF REGIONAL HISTORY

• The Arawaks and the Caribs
• The Conquest
• Bitter Sugar
• African Resistance to Slavery
• Emancipation and Free Village Life
• From India to the Caribbean
• The Promise of Education
• Antillean Independence Movements
• Gunboat Diplomacy
• The Cuban Revolution
• West Indian Independence
• Sources of Classroom Materials

Caribbean Connections:
JAMAICA

❝A superb introduction to Jamaican history and culture: concise, yet accurate and comprehensive. This book is an excellent resource for all school systems which have a serious concern for multicultural education.❞

— E. Leopold Edwards
Council of Caribbean Organizations of the Greater Washington and Baltimore Metropolitan Areas

Highlights of JAMAICA

• Jamaica at a Glance
• A Brief History of Jamaica
• Anansi, Brer Rabbit and the Folk Tradition
• Our Jamaican Heritage
• The Marcus Garvey Movement
• Louise Bennett, National Poetess of Jamaica
• In the Country
• From Rasta to Reggae
• Women's Theater in Jamaica
• Sources of Classroom Materials

Caribbean Connections:
PUERTO RICO

❝Here are the voices of Puerto Rican workers, women, activists, writers and musicians. Puerto Rican students will find their heritage presented here with knowledge and dignity. Students and teachers of other backgrounds will enjoy a wonderful and informed introduction to Puerto Rican life today.❞

— Dr. Rina Benmayor
Center for Puerto Rican Studies, Hunter College

Highlights of PUERTO RICO

• Puerto Rico at a Glance
• A Brief History of Puerto Rico
• A Lead Box that Couldn't Be Opened*
• Memories of Puerto Rico and New York*
• La Bomba and La Plena, Music of Puerto Rico*
• The Customs and Traditions of the Tabaqueros
• Arturo Alfonso Schomburg
• Our Mothers' Struggle Has Shown Us the Way
• Operation Bootstrap's Legacy
• Vieques and the Navy
• What Future for Puerto Rico?
• Sources of Classroom Materials   * Includes texts in Spanish.

Caribbean Connections is a project of the **Ecumenical Program on Central America and the Caribbean** (**EPICA**) and the **Network of Educators on the Americas** (**NECA**). It is funded in part by the **D.C. Community Humanities Council**, **The CarEth Foundation**, and the **Anita Mishler Education Fund**.

Caribbean Connections

• OVERVIEW OF REGIONAL HISTORY • PUERTO RICO • JAMAICA •

Series Advisors

Judy Aaronson
Staff Development Division
District of Columbia
Public Schools

Dr. Rina Benmayor
Center for Puerto Rican Studies
Hunter College

Honor Ford-Smith
Sistren Theatre Collective of
Jamaica

Lori Kaplan
Latin American Youth Center
Washington, D.C.

Dr. Linda Mauro
School of Education
The George Washington University

Dr. Brenda Gayle Plummer
Department of Afro-American
History
University of Minnesota

Dr. Deloris Saunders
School of Education
The George Washington University

Dr. Constance Sutton
Department of Anthropology
New York University

Dr. Michel-Rolph Trouillot
Department of Anthropology
The Johns Hopkins University

Dr. Keith Warner
Department of Foreign
Languages and Literatures
George Mason University

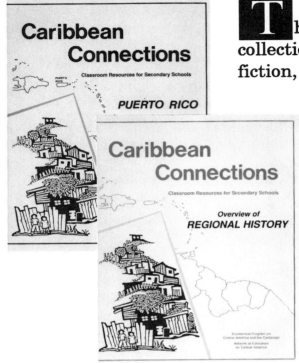

These lively illustrated collections present fiction, non-fiction, oral histories, interviews, map exercises, poetry, drama and songs.

Each unit includes a teacher's guide with background information, objectives, discussion questions, and suggested activities.

Excellent for secondary schools, colleges and community groups.

Ideal for Social Studies, English, Spanish, and Global Studies classes.

ORDER FORM

Return this form to: NECA, 1118 22nd Street, NW, Washington, D.C. 20037. Postage and handling is $3 for each title, or $5 for two to six titles. For bulk discounts and other information, please inquire at (202) 429-0137 or (202) 429-9766 (FAX). Make checks payable to NECA.

Please send me:

☐ Overview of Regional History $15.95 (ISBN # 1-878554-06-9)

☐ Jamaica $12.00 (ISBN # 1-878554-05-0)

☐ Puerto Rico $12.00 (ISBN # 1-878554-04-2)

Please notify me when the following are available:

☐ Caribbean Life in North America

☐ Haiti

Name: _____

Organization: _____

Address: _____

City: _____ State: _____ Zip: _____ Telephone: _____

Position: _____ Subject: _____ Grade: _____
(If educator)

Teacher Notes